C-3PO

TALES OF THE GOLDEN DROID

EBURY
PRESS

C-3PO

TALES OF THE GOLDEN DROID

By Daniel Wallace and Josh Ling

Ebury Press
Random House, 20 Vauxhall Bridge Road, London SW1V 2SA

The Random House Group Limited Reg. No. 954009

A CIP catalogue record for this book is available from the British Library

ISBN: 0 09 1873576

Coordinated by Lucy Autrey Wilson (Lucasfilm)
Edited by Allan Kausch (Lucasfilm) and Sarah Malarkey (Chronicle Books)

Book design by Tolleson Design
Design direction by Michael Carabetta and Julia Flagg

Printed in China

Acknowledgments

This second in the series of *Star Wars* Masterpiece Edition books couldn't have been done without the help and consultation of Steve
Sansweet, who provided generously of his time as well as photos of his collection.

At Lucasfilm thanks once again go to Lucy Autrey Wilson, Director of Publishing; Allan Kausch, Continuity Editor; and Tina Mills,
Cara Evangelista, and Halina Krukowski, for help with images. At Chronicle Books, thanks to editor Sarah Malarkey, design experts
Julia Flagg and Michael Carabetta, and Mikyla Bruder.

The C-3PO collectibles in this book were photographed by Steve Essig.

This book is dedicated to the "real world" C-3Po, Anthony Daniels, a solid gold actor to *Star Wars* fans everywhere.

TABLE OF CONTENTS

110100111010000011100101000111011011110110101010101010100010001100011100111010001110100000011100101010001110110011000111
010101010100100011000111010011101000000011
001110100111010000011100101000111011011110110101010101010010010010101011101101001000010101010101001010110

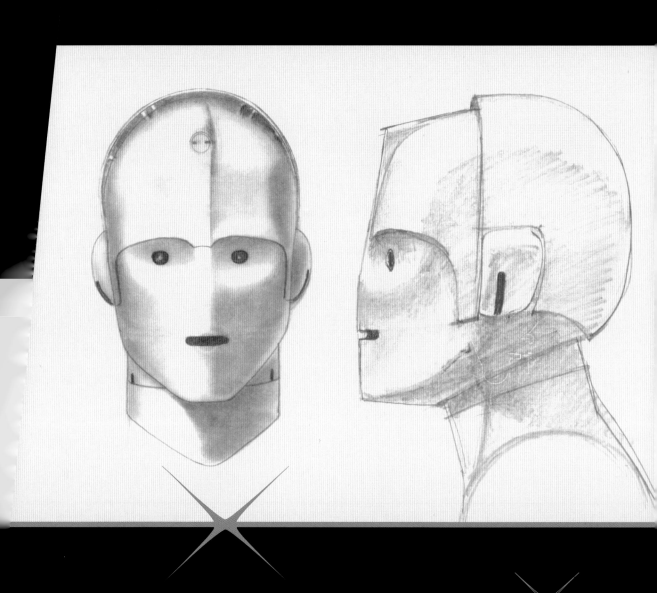

I: THE BIRTH OF THE GOLDEN DROID

It wasn't the grandest entrance in film history, but the golden robot with a humanoid look had a certain endearing, all-too-human quality about him as he stiffly shuffled about the deck of the large spacecraft and communicated with a squat counterpart who spoke only in electronic beeps and whistles. That quality translated into true stardom for what the movie-going public would learn were not robots but droids, C-3PO and R2-D2 to be exact. They were designed as the viewport through which the entire *Star Wars* saga was to be seen, and if that role was later diminished, they still had another equally important task. The two droids, one tall and fussy, one short and smart, were the saga's comic relief, the Laurel and Hardy of the droid world.

It's quite enough for a fictional character to be introduced even once to the public in so distinctive a manner. But See-Threepio has now had the honor twice. Some twenty-two years after the droid first appeared, George Lucas—by going back in time and making a new series of films that predates the classic *Star Wars* trilogy—has shown C-3PO's origins at the hands of a talented young Anakin Skywalker. If, in order to do that, Lucas reworked some past *Star Wars* quasi-gospel, it only proves that the creator is constantly tinkering with the galaxy he created. "Always in motion is the future," a small green Jedi Master once said. To Yoda's words of wisdom, George Lucas might add: And so is the past.

The personalities of the two droids were apparent in an instant. *American Cinematographer*, in its classic July 1977 *Star Wars* issue, described Threepio as "a fussy British-accented pessimist. His pint-size buddy, Artoo-Detoo, built like a hand grenade, is a spunky little computerized scrapper. They almost steal the picture from the human characters."

Opposite: Concept designer Ralph McQuarrie's early sketches of C-3PO's head were different from the final version, especially in the area of the droid's eyes.

Left: We first meet C-3PO, in story terms, in Star Wars: Episode I The Phantom Menace. *He is an unfinished protocol droid that Anakin Skywalker is building. This design by concept artist Doug Chiang was turned into reality at Industrial Light & Magic.*

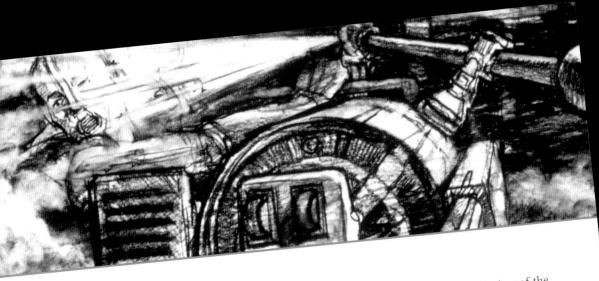

In reality, they almost didn't make it at all. Lucas has long been an ardent admirer of the works of legendary Japanese film director Akira Kurosawa, and he was strongly influenced by the epic *The Hidden Fortress* when structuring *Star Wars*. As Laurent Bouzereau explains in his fascinating book, *Star Wars: The Annotated Screenplays*, *The Hidden Fortress* is about a princess who escapes from an enemy with the aid of her faithful commander. Disguised as peasants, and with a fortune in gold hidden amidst firewood, they set out on a dangerous journey with the help of two unpolished farmers who hope to get some of the gold.

In the first treatment of *Star Wars*, the now familiar droids were nowhere to be seen. Instead, for comic relief, Lucas had two bungling Imperial bureaucrats who were patterned after Kurosawa's farmers. The droids quickly surfaced aboard the Death Star in the rough draft of what was then called *The Star Wars*.

"You focus on the human story first, and then you begin to create this world that everybody inhabits, and playing with the lowest person in the hierarchy, I created droids," Lucas told Bouzereau. "I was looking for the lowest person on the pecking order, basically like the farmers in *Hidden Fortress* were."

The writer-director then decided that the story would be told from the droids' vantage point. "The part that was the most interesting in *Hidden Fortress* was that it was told from the point of view of the farmers, and not from the point of view of the princess. I liked that idea. It set me off on a very interesting course because it really did frame the movie in a very interesting way and altered the point of view of all three movies," he told Bouzereau.

Right: One of McQuarrie's first poster concept paintings features a more feminine C-3PO as well as a girl in the role that would become Luke Skywalker.

0001100011101001110100000111100101000111011011110110101010101010100100101010101
1010010100100100100101000101000111011011110110101010101010100100101

In the first rough draft dated May 1974, the droids weren't introduced until Scene
35, and Artoo-Detoo (then spelled differently) actually spoke in words.

35. SUB-HALLWAY—IMPERIAL SPACE FORTRESS

*Constant explosions rock the interior of the fortress. Civilians, including women and children, scurry for
safety in the panic-ridden hallways. Two construction robots, Artwo Detwo (R2D2) and See Threepio
(C3Po), are blown, slipping and sliding across the hallway floor into some freight canisters. Both robots are
rather old and battered. Artwo is a short, (three feet) claw-armed tri-pod. His face is a mass of computer
lights, surrounding a radar eye. Threepio is a tall, gleaming android of human proportions. He is thin, with
a totally metallic surface of an art deco design. The robots attempt to get out from under the canisters, but
rushing gas from a broken pipe keeps knocking them over.*

THREEPIO   This is madness; we're going to be destroyed. I'm still not accustomed
to space travel.

ARTWO   The external bombardment does appear to be concentrated in this area.
The structure has exceeded the normal stress quotient by point four,
although there appears to be no immediate danger.

THREEPIO   No immediate danger! You're faulty. This is madness!

Below: C-3PO is thrown to the floor of a starship under attack in this early storyboard by Alex Tavoularis.

Right: In this version of the script and storyboards, it is C-3PO who bravely takes charge of the escape of himself and the reluctant R2-D2.

Opposite below: "You stay," Threepio badgers Artoo. "I'm going to eject before the whole thing goes up."

00100101010110110100
)100100110001010001110110111101101010101010100100101010110110100

Artwo gives Threepio a sheepish look and clings to a side rail for dear life, as debris flies through the hallway.

When looking at early drafts of any work, it's fun and sometimes instructive to see what has changed. A few scenes after the one above, it is C-3PO not R2-D2 who makes the decision to use escape pods when their ship is exploding. In fact, "Artwo" staunchly resists, showing some of the characteristics that would later be assigned to the droid Han Solo nicknamed "Goldenrod."

41. SUB-HALLWAYS—IMPERIAL SPACE FORTRESS
The impact of the exploding starship can be felt throughout the giant fortress. The tall, gleaming Threepio races through several corridors, yelling at Artwo, who struggles vainly to keep pace with his stubby mechanical feet.

THREEPIO	. . . I don't care what you do, but I'm getting out. All the power's out. Those explosions are coming from the reactor section. This is the end. Abandon ship.
ARTWO	Our work—we can't leave! It's desertion. It's not possible. It's not possible.
THREEPIO	Your programming is so limited. My first order is preservation. You stay. I'm going to eject before the whole thing goes up.

Threepio breaks open the seal on an emergency lifepod. A red warning light begins to flash, and a low hum is heard. The lanky chrome android works his way into the cramped four-man craft.

> **ARTWO**　　These lifepods aren't for us! It's not right!

A new explosion, this time very close, sends dust and debris through the narrow passageway. Flames lick at the two robots. The runt-sized Artwo jumps into the lifepod.

> **ARTWO**　　It's the end. Eject. Eject.

The safety door snaps shut, and the pod ejects from the fortress.

By the second draft, there had been something of a role reversal. Bouzereau discovered that Lucas' notes pegged Artoo as a staunchly loyal servant, puppylike and naive, but very bright. His speech became a series of electronic sounds. "Threepio, by contrast, is a coward, greedy and a fast talker, almost a con man."

"I remember at some point it seemed dramatically more interesting to me to have both droids talk, but it took some of the mystery, charm, and uniqueness out of the characters," Lucas recalled. "The idea was to make them different, have them bounce off of each other to identify them easily as separate characters. I tried to make them as opposite as possible." At that point, Lucas planned to have Threepio sound oily, something like a used car dealer from Brooklyn. "I had an idea of more of

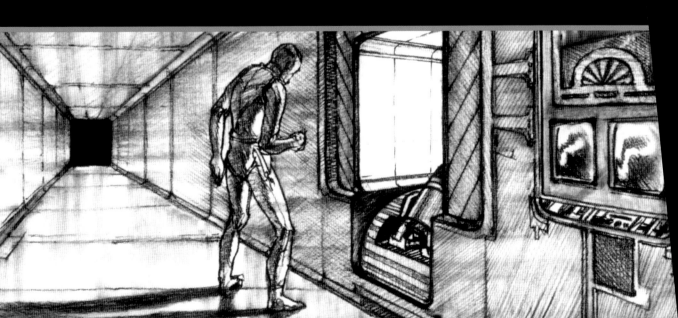

Below: C-3PO and R2-D2 helped present a Special Achievement Academy Award for Sound Effects to Ben Burtt at the 1978 Oscar show. The film received six other Oscars.

Opposite: The golden droid has a face that can show some emotion in this early sketch by Alex Tavoularis.

C-3PO: TALES OF THE GOLDEN DROID

a con man, which is the way it was written, and not a sort of fussy British robot butler," he said. But British actor Anthony Daniels not only filled Threepio's suit perfectly, he *became* Threepio.

Actually, it wasn't just Anthony Daniels' voice by itself—or those of foreign voice actors in the dubbed version of *Star Wars*. Academy Award–winning sound designer Ben Burtt—who created the unforgettable breathing sound of Darth Vader—also had a role.

"For Threepio's voice, generally we tried to achieve a metallic effect, which we have been able to get in the past by taking two identical copies of the voice and playing them slightly out of sync so that you get a phasing between them," Burtt said. "There's a certain point in the phasing where you get a metallic characteristic, and this is what we always tried to achieve with Threepio.

"We always wanted to be subtle about it because we didn't want him to become too 'inhuman.' We wanted all the emotion and animation in his voice that we could get, yet we wanted something qualitatively about the voice to be slightly machine-like."

Because Anthony Daniels' accent and inflection in his delivery of Threepio's lines was such an important part of the characterization of the droid, Lucasfilm had to carefully cast foreign voices for the film's dubbed versions.

"In *Star Wars*, the most important thing about the translation is the relationship between the droids, Threepio especially, and humans," noted Gary Kurtz, the film's producer, in a previously unpublished interview. "In English it was no real problem. Threepio has a special sound. He is a fussy English butler in the Jeeves tradition, but that is a very cultural thing. It's not something that you can automatically translate to another language, especially one that doesn't have tonal differences like that that you can use." In Italy, for example, Threepio was given a Northern Italian, somewhat upper-class accent while the rest of the voiceover actors had more or less neutral Roman accents to make Threepio's different enough to stand out.

Many fans know the story of how part of the droid duo got its name. Lucas was at a sound recording session for *American Graffiti* when sound editor Walter Murch asked someone to go to the rack and get R2-D2—reel two, dialogue track two. The director liked the sound of that and wrote it down in a small notebook he carried for when inspiration struck. Alas, there's no equally compelling anecdote for Threepio. Lucas says he just played around with sounds and words phonetically, and after he spoke a name aloud many times, if it sounded right, it stuck.

One compelling reason for the droid presence in the *Star Wars* saga was that they contrasted so well with the evil of the Galactic Empire, particularly its emissary, Darth Vader. "Having machines, like the droids, that are reasonably compassionate, and a man like Vader who becomes a machine and loses his compassion was a theme that interested me," Lucas told Bouzereau.

The physical appearance of C-3PO was the effort of several people. George Lucas had the initial idea and a mental picture of his metallic droid. Concept artist and production illustrator Ralph McQuarrie was given the task of turning Lucas' ideas into two-dimensional reality, first through sketches and then an early pre-production painting. A handful of such paintings convinced the reluctant directors of Twentieth Century Fox that this strange film might not be a total bust. It then fell to art director Norman Reynolds and sculptress Liz Moore to turn McQuarrie's flat art into three-dimensional reality.

Opposite: These extended torso and nearly full-body sketches by Ralph McQuarrie were partially inspired by the robot Maria from the German silent film Metropolis.

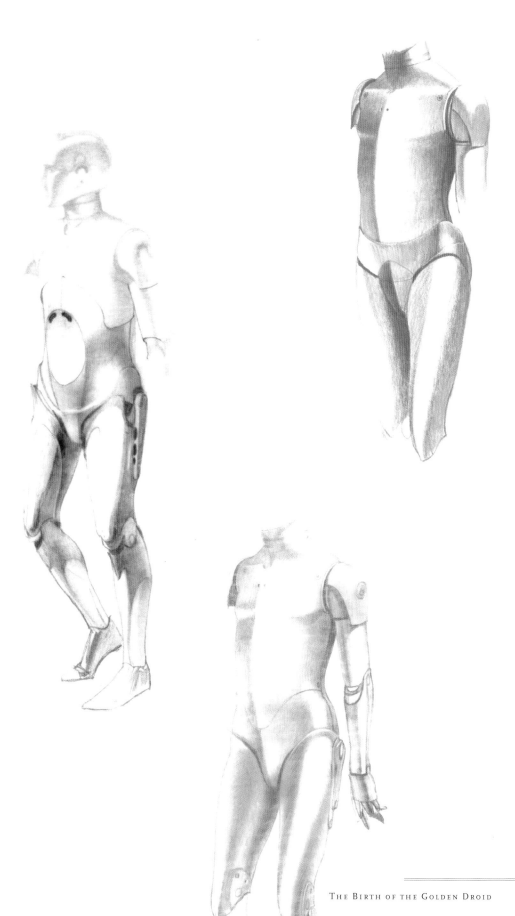

THE BIRTH OF THE GOLDEN DROID

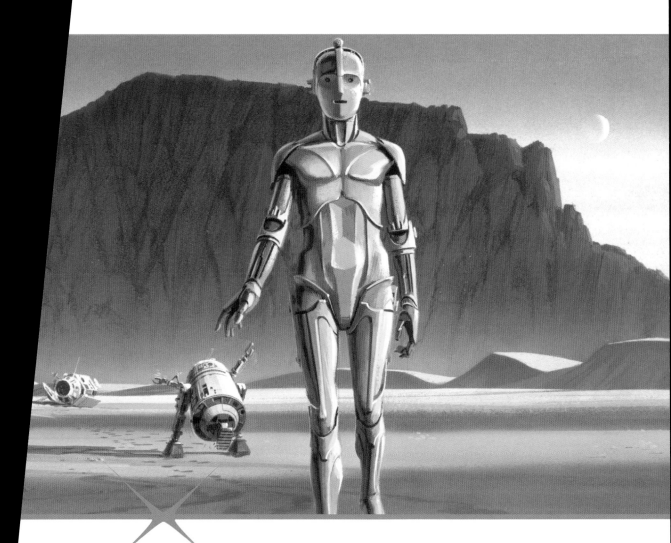

This early look at C-3PO and R2-D2 was in one of the
first batches of pre-production paintings that Ralph
McQuarrie turned out to help George Lucas convince
Twentieth Century Fox to give the go-ahead to Star Wars.

C-3PO: TALES OF THE GOLDEN DROID

"One of the things that thrilled me about working with George was that he didn't just stop by my apartment and tell me how to do everything, what shape everything should be and what color," McQuarrie recalled. "In fact, he and Gary [Kurtz, the film's producer] just brought the script by one day and left it with me. They said read the script and when you come to something you think you'd like to illustrate—some kind of scene—make a note of it and we'll talk about it later and you'll make some little sketches or something."

Lucas ripped drawings out of magazines, comic books, or illustrated novels to give McQuarrie an idea of the direction he wanted. "My recollection is that he brought in pictures of the robot from *Metropolis* to give me some inspiration." McQuarrie's first turn was giving Threepio "very delicate lines and smooth surfaces" like a sculpture by pop artist Ernest Trova. During the 1960s and 1970s Trova's sculptures in polished stainless steel and bronze of machine-like anonymous people with featureless faces and interchangeable body parts had brought him prominence in the United States.

In the end, the look of Threepio clearly paid homage to the visionary German director Fritz Lang and his visually stunning if plot-impaired 1926 silent black-and-white tour de force, *Metropolis.* In the film, half of the population are oppressed underground worker drones, in perpetual thrall to the pampered populace that lives aboveground. Their only inspiration is a beautiful woman named Maria. Demented scientist Rotwang constructs a robot, captures Maria, and transfers her face to the android so that the workers can be fooled and remain under control.

In early sketches and the first pre-production paintings, McQuarrie's Threepio was similar to Lang's Maria, with a face and metallic anatomy that was definitely feminine. "George said to

Below: Production Designer John Barry did a number of simple line drawings to try to come up with a concept that would work for Threepio's face.

Opposite: Liz Moore sculpted a number of clay heads to try to come up with a fixed design that could work with all emotions.

make it look more like a boy," the artist recalled. There was also a practical reason that such a graceful and slim vision of Threepio wouldn't work. The need to have an actor inside the suit for hours on end made it imperative that the droid's body be bigger and have larger joints. A sidelight on the now famous painting, which also shows an earlier version of R2-D2: McQuarrie based his landscape on a sweeping photograph of the Oregon coast. He followed the line of the dramatic cliff, but replaced crashing ocean waves with sand dunes.

"I wanted something elegant and beautiful and human-like with Threepio, so I was inspired primarily by the film *Metropolis,* which was one of the first films I ever saw with a robot in it," Lucas told Jane Paley, who interviewed him for a film and audio tour that accompanied the yearlong *Star Wars: The Magic of Myth* exhibition at the Smithsonian Institution's National Air and Space Museum. "The robot in that film was very art deco, very beautiful. A lot of the art deco elements in Threepio relate to the ribbing on the legs, and the fixtures, like in his head, have a sort of series of little donuts put together in descending order, which is a very art deco image."

But why does "Goldenrod" have one silver leg? "I made that leg silver so that Threepio could have a history, so it looked like he had been around for twenty or thirty years, so it looked like he had some adventures and somebody had taken a leg off and replaced it," Lucas said.

Actually, Goldenrod wasn't pre-ordained to be golden. "We thought about Threepio being slick chrome, sort of like the chrome robots in *THX 1138,*" Lucas said in a previously unpublished interview. "I like chrome—the shine of it—but then we decided that Threepio was really the more human of the robots and we'd make him part of the human contingent, which for the heroes is almost all flesh and brown and beige colors."

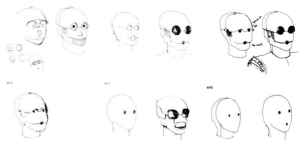

Turning the Threepio design into three-dimensional reality wasn't like dusting crops, as one rogue starship pilot would tell young hero Luke Skywalker. Even production designer John Barry had a hand in it.

"What we did for the face was very important," Barry said in a previously unpublished 1977 interview. "You're going to be stuck with somebody's constant expression all the way through the movie. The robot from *Metropolis* has a very benign female face, but George had this concept of what his droid should look like. So I did a lot of very simple line drawings of different expressions, sometimes the difference just being how two dots [Threepio's eyes] were placed on the face. That's when George decided he wanted to go for a slightly humorous, slightly silly look and Liz Moore sculpted it."

Moore, who sculpted the Star Child for *2001: A Space Odyssey* while still a teenager and worked with *Star Wars* production designer Barry on *A Clockwork Orange*, actually sculpted nine different Threepio heads in clay. "We stood them up at head height all the way around the stage so that George could look at one without looking at them all," Barry said. "They were kept well apart so they didn't interfere with one another. George could stare at each one and decide which one said to him what he wanted it to say as far as the look."

Lucas settled on one of the sculpted heads, but it still wasn't quite right. He took a couple of coins from his pocket and stuck them on over the smaller dots that were the droid's eyes. He also wanted changes to the mouth, so Moore poked into the clay and resculpted the mouth while the director looked on. "There's not a line in *Star Wars* that doesn't have George's influence," Barry added. Tragically, Moore was killed in a traffic accident in the Netherlands the year before the space fantasy opened. She never saw how much audiences appreciated her artistry.

"One great thing about working with the robots," noted Richard Chew, one of the film's editors, "was that since there wasn't any lip-sync problem for an editor to worry about, we just chose whatever we wanted that looked good and then we could 'cheat in' anything else. For See-Threepio we had at least the guide track for Tony Daniels, the production track where he's speaking underneath the mask, although very muffled."

Today it is impossible to think of one of the world's most famous nonhuman characters without thinking of the man in the golden suit. Anthony Daniels, the young British actor who was selected to play C-3PO, so infused the role and created the golden droid's personality that the two have become inseparable in the public's mind. And although Threepio has only a small role in *Star Wars:* Episode I, there was no doubt that Daniels would once again supply his voice and persona as the droid's origins and his first meeting with R2-D2 unfolded.

Over the years, Daniels has played Threepio in many venues, from books on tape to appearances at fan conventions. He has given hundreds of interviews and written dozens of columns and magazine articles. But his first extensive interview, done several months before *Star Wars* opened in May 1977, has gathered dust in the Lucasfilm Library archives for more than two decades. It was conducted by then–Lucasfilm marketing executive Charlie Lippincott for a possible book, and it sparkles with Daniels' self-deprecating wit and the freshness of anecdotes being told for the first time. Here, in a slightly edited form and in only one of Threepio's six million forms of galactic languages, is the heart of the interview.

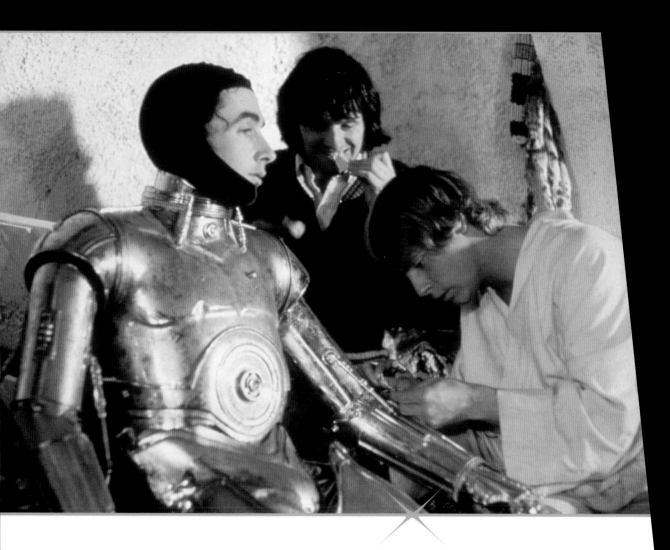

Left: A partially costumed Anthony Daniels takes direction from a young George Lucas in the Tunisian desert.

Above: There were continual problems with the C-3PO costume. Sometimes even fellow actor Mark Hamill helped piece Anthony Daniels' suit back together.

"One very nice thing about playing such a big part completely hidden was that I could observe how filming was done with a certain amount of safety, without making an idiot of myself," Daniels told Lippincott.

"It came about when my agent rang up, and she said there was this man called George Lucas making a space fantasy. Do you want to go and see him? She said they were very interested in me because I'm good at mime. She talked a lot about the film and, the only trouble was, the part was a robot. So I said, 'Oh, come on now, I'm a serious actor. We've got to get on with my career, don't we?'

"So two or three months later, I went to Fox London headquarters. I looked at George and I must say that I immediately liked him. But we greeted each other and then there was silence. Fortunately for both of us, the [McQuarrie] production paintings were on the wall facing George. So I turned to the pictures and asked him about them, and I must say that he opened up and became quite dynamic. His excitement spilled over to me and it was about an hour later when my meeting ended."

Daniels got the script a few days later and took a long time reading it through. And then read it again. "After reading it three times, I wrote out the story in sections and then I got to under-stand vaguely what it was about. I think it was like an intelligence test. Any actor who could get through the script—with its strange character and place names and even weirder descriptions—was allowed to meet George for the second time.

"I became very excited about the character. I immediately realized that C-3PO was not an ordinary robot, and I began to forget all of my original ideas of playing one. I went back to George with

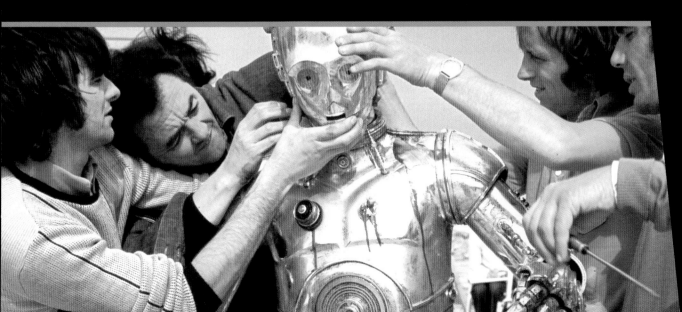

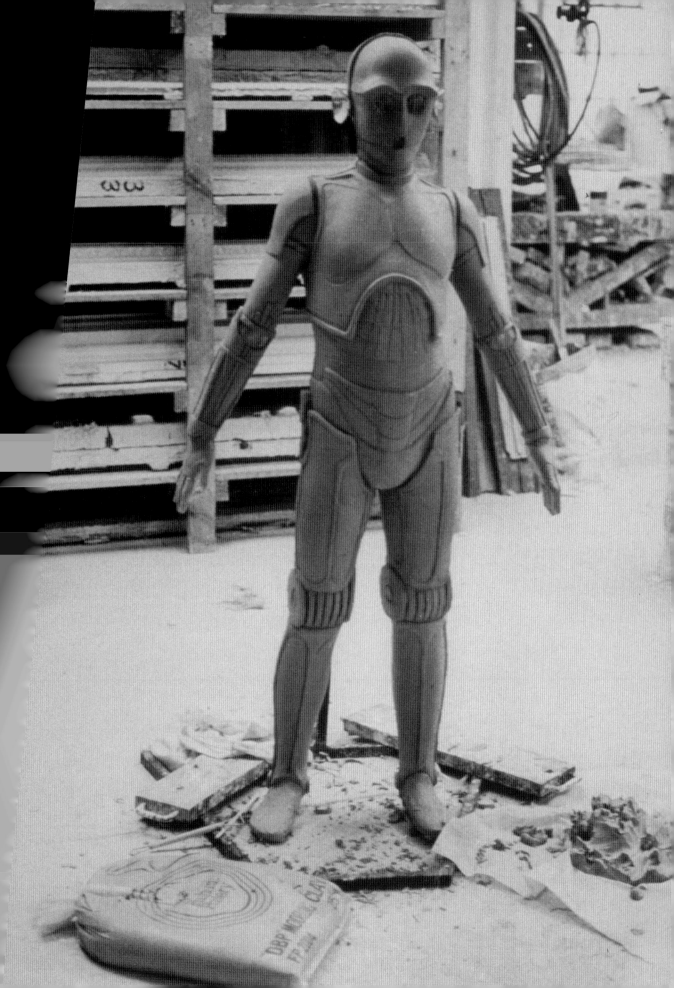

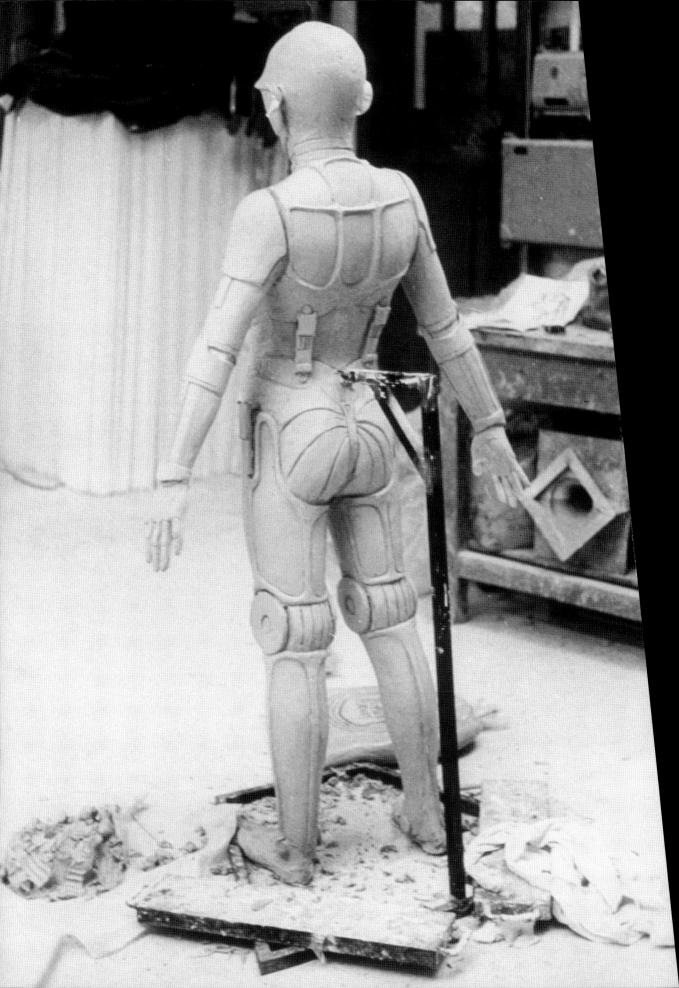

some notes I'd written, but most of the things I'd planned were impossible once I was wearing the suit." On his second interview, not knowing that Lucas had already picked him, Daniels did most of the talking. After about an hour, and still unsure whether he had the role, he told Lucas that he'd really like the part. "Sure," the director replied. "It was like winning a prize," Daniels recalled, and it was especially sweet since he was one of the first actors cast.

That buzz didn't last for long, since his first assignment was to get his body cast to make a mold for the costume. "The glamour of films really hit the dirt when these two laborers came up with buckets of plaster and Vaseline, and I'm standing there cold and shivering with practically nothing on. First they did my feet, which was all right because I could sit down for that. Then they did the whole back of me in one piece and then they put the front on. It was one of the most disgusting experiences of my life.

"They were very worried about doing my head because they said a lot of people faint and collapse. But I said I'd be fine so they stuck a couple of straws up my nose and they did the back of my head first. Then they painted over one eye, then over the other one, then over my mouth. And gradually it began to be the most beautiful experience because my head was then surrounded by three inches of plaster and nobody could get at me. I felt totally safe and secure—talk about back to the womb! I just lay there in absolute darkness. What is very sinister about it is that when the mask is removed from the face all the wrinkles and blemishes of your face are in it."

Actually, Daniels had to undergo a body cast a second time since the first one twisted in on itself because of the weight. But things improved when he met Liz Moore. "When she arrived the film began to look up for me because she was interested, and she was the person who sculpted C-3PO,

in fact created it. Liz was a love and she could see how uncomfortable it was for me, and made sure that I was as comfortable as possible. So there was this very beautiful woman and there was I wearing ladies' tights and the rest of me wrapped in sandwich foil. Then she was slapping great jars of Nivea all over me to stop the plaster from slipping. Some of the laborers remarked that they could tell I hadn't shaved, and I could tell they didn't mean my face. And we had to cast the hands four times."

The suit was eventually made, but not before some experimentation with different materials. "They made the whole suit in rubber, which must have cost the earth, and I would have cooked in that," Daniels said. "George and Gary kept coming in and spending the whole day fiddling around with my elbow or my knee or my shoulder, trying to work out how to make this garb work for a robot. They finally hit on specially engineered wheels and rings that fit together beautifully."

All the development work took so long, however, that the first time Daniels put on the full final costume was on the first day of filming in Tunisia. It took two hours. "By the time I walked ten paces out of the tent on the Tunisian salt flats, it hurt so much that I felt I couldn't make it to the set about three hundred yards away," Daniels recalled. "I felt I wasn't going to make it through the film, but I kind of hobbled and lurched over to the set and we began filming.

"I was wearing ordinary nylon leotards and some very nasty little sailing shoes that got very battered. Those were under gold shoes, under the gold legs, which went up into a pair of trousers that bolted together at the hips and had a rather large crotch. And then I had a kind of corset in the middle which was made of very thick rubber and sewed by hand. It had lots of spare wires and junk that, during the course of the film, changes incredibly. Fitting above those is a front and back piece. The front piece contains the left arm hole and the back piece contains the right. Then the whole thing fits together like a jigsaw with me in the middle."

It was a very tight fit. "It was precision engineered, and if I got in it the wrong way I got very badly cut up," Daniels said. "Two bolts would go into the neck. It was also bolted just above the waist and there was no way on earth I could get out of that thing. I was a prisoner! The arms were slid up and hooked on the shoulder. The hands were gloves specially made by another sculptor, who decided they should be made in sheet steel. Sheet steel—crazy! The first time I put them on, I could hold up a hand for about twenty seconds before it would clunk on a table. I said they had to make me something else."

Daniels had nothing but praise for sculptress Moore. "She did the body, the feet, and the head," he remembered. "There were some very pretty masks and some very noble looking ones. Of course, I wanted to look pretty *and* noble, and in the end the right one was chosen. It's a terrific face and it has great adaptability: it has so many expressions. It's hard to say why it works, but it does."

The rest of the costume, however, was an engineering nightmare. "It was a full-time problem right through the film, and [art director] Norman Reynolds had to work a lot of overtime because of me. George and Gary pitched in too. We'd make cardboard mock-ups of shoulder pieces and then get engineers to make them and they wouldn't work, and then we'd have to get something else made. I also had a couple of tapes around my chest to hold on the front of the costume, which was very heavy, and that made breathing extremely difficult."

Difficulties with the costume as well as the conception of the role led to Threepio's mime-

Right: With limited vision and mobility, Anthony Daniels couldn't move very far in the sand dunes of Tunisia without considerable assistance.

like movements. "Obviously he couldn't walk like a human; that would be silly. So it was a cross between that thought and the problems of the costume. Some days it would go on well, and some days I could barely move. I also had a very limited field of vision, completely tunnel-like."

So, is it any wonder that Threepio came off as more than a bit fussy, even petulant? The man trapped inside the golden coffin was being pinched and scratched and cut continuously. But there's much more to Daniels' characterization than that.

"It's a terrific character," Daniels said. "He's kind of a cross between an English butler and Laurel and Hardy, with his friend R2-D2. One of the things about being inside him was that whatever you're doing, you can react as much as you like and nobody will notice. If I were emotionally upset in a scene, or angry or excited, I would be those things inside my costume. I was smiling at the end when Luke comes to get his medal. I played it a bit like a Jewish mama seeing her son at his bar mitzvah. Of course you really can't see that, but a lot of things did come through in the movement of the rest of my body, so I think it was very important. It's a lot like radio acting, where people are emotional and physically move around because it's the only way to make yourself believable.

"This unlikely shape has all the human attributes it could have and more. It seems outlandish because he isn't human. You take for granted when you look at somebody's face that you know what they're up to. You have to think about it with a robot, and you're taken by surprise with it."

Threepio is constantly in action, even if it's only cocking his head or raising an arm. "What George could instantly spot was that I only existed when I moved. If I didn't move, the voice could be coming from anywhere. So I very carefully had to think out how to move as I spoke, sort of

Above: An Alex Tavoularis storyboard sketch shows early versions of the two droids aboard a Rebel cruiser.

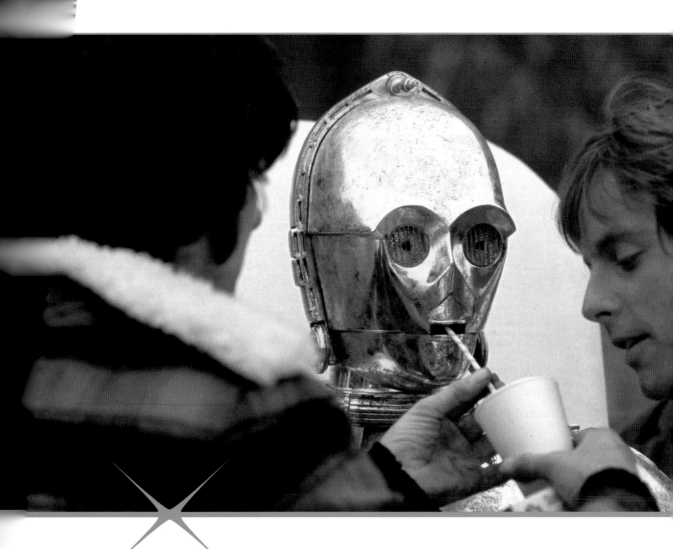

Above: Even getting a sip of liquid refreshment during the shooting of Star Wars was a task that took the help of several others, including Luke Skywalker himself.

Right: Once locked inside his C-3PO suit, actor Anthony Daniels couldn't sit down; he could only lean against a backboard, which occasionally also served as a mode of transport with the help of several stagehands.

10101001000010111100101010101010010101

speak the lines with my head, physically. Another problem was that when human beings talk to each other, they look each other in the eyes to help determine what they're thinking. People would vaguely look at me somewhere around my left cheek or just above my eyebrow, but never in the eyes."

Even simple actions required lots of patience, and sometimes lots of takes. "There's a magical shot in the film where you see my hand come into the shot and pick up a comlink. It took about twenty attempts to do that, and then the only way was to put a sticky pad in the palm of my hand. I had to watch very carefully out of camera as the sticky pad came somewhat close to its target. Every day was a new experience."

One of the ironies for Daniels is that even while he successfully infused humanity into a mechanical thing, on the set the opposite seemed to be happening. "After a while, people would completely forget there was a human being inside the robot suit, and they would say things within my sight and hearing that they obviously wouldn't have said otherwise, and they would leave me out of things. Nobody on the film quite knew who I was for a long time."

Near the start of filming Daniels saw a director's chair with his name stenciled on the back. "I got very excited about it, but I never saw it after that. I never got to sit in the chair because I could never sit down. I had this terrible leaning board, a kind of medieval thing with arms that allow you to recline at about seventy degrees, and it was very little use at all because the weight still went down to my ankles, sort of like walking around with a great barbell. I said that the board should have had C-3PO painted on the back because nobody knew who I was, but they knew who this gold fellow was."

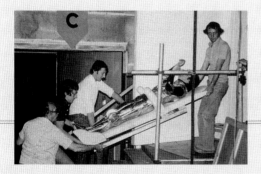

0001101110010010100010100011101110100111010000011110010100001110010010100100000101001100101000010

For all the problems the role brought, Daniels wouldn't have traded it for the world. How much he and the character merged can be seen in one telling incident. While Daniels did some stunts, others were ruled too dangerous. "I was sorry I didn't do the stunt where I fall off the cliff, because we spent a lot of time dressing someone else and then all he did was fall ninety degrees. I felt sure I could have done that. Also, I didn't like the idea of somebody playing my part. I mean, C-3PO, by this time, thoroughly belonged to me and no one else was getting a piece of the action. I've become very fond of him."

As has the rest of the world. When it came time to do U.S. public service television spots warning youngsters about the dangers of smoking, who better a spokesdroid than Threepio? An immunization campaign in Australia? Footprints in the wet cement at Mann's Chinese Theater in Hollywood? The golden one once again. Of course, there was the time that he appeared on a tram poster advertising a pub on the Isle of Man in Great Britain. And the Polish poster for *Star Wars*, while featuring C-3PO, also looked like a flock of birds had done to him what they normally do to car windshields. You can just hear him exclaim, "Oh my!"

In his adaptation of Episode I, novelist Terry Brooks tells how the CPO-class protocol droid was named by the precocious Anakin Skywalker. "He'd given it a number the night before, choosing "three" because the droid made the third member of his little family after his mother and himself." Countless *Star Wars* fans have long wished that this fully drawn character, a mechanical man who seems so real and only too human, was a member of their own family.

Right: Marking a special moment in Star Wars *history, C-3PO and R2-D2 celebrate the film's first birthday in this publicity shot. Even after a year, the film was still playing in a number of American theaters.*

II: THE SAGA OF SEE-THREEPIO

Machines with personalities. Hardware that thinks. Artificial intelligence is a very old invention indeed, dating back tens of thousands of years to the days of the conqueror Xim the Despot. It is surprising, then, that so much prejudice exists towards robots, automatons, and other mechanicals, collectively referred to as droids. Under galactic law, droids are property, not self-aware beings in their own right. Amateur philosophers may insist that the intelligence of droids is an illusion and their emotions a sham, and thus they are not truly "alive." It's a safe bet that none of these naysayers has ever made the acquaintance of a golden droid with the alphanumeric designation of C-3PO.

See-Threepio, or Threepio as most call him, is a protocol droid specializing in diplomacy and etiquette. His features include a microwave emitter, an energy transducer, and a database containing more than six million languages. But Threepio is much more than the sum of his parts. He is a motherly fussbudget who can be quick with a cruel put-down. He is a slick fast-talker, yet honest to the point of being naive. He is a panicky coward, yet one of the bravest beings you'll ever meet. In short, he is as complicated and contradictory as any human being, and possesses a patient, noble dignity that puts most humans to shame.

Many details of See-Threepio's early operational life are still a mystery, but his "birth" can be definitively traced to the desert planet Tatooine, more than a generation before the Battle of Yavin. Anakin Skywalker, then a nine-year-old slave owned by Watto the Toydarian, began tinkering with parts he had salvaged from Watto's junkyard. The boy had an innate gift for mechanics and hoped to build a protocol droid to assist his mother with chores and errands. Anakin had collected a number of discarded protocol components, but a working cognitive module eluded him. A droid brain was far too

THE SAGA OF SEE-THREEPIO

valuable to be left lying in a scrapheap. Amazingly, Anakin was able to splice together a full personality matrix from burnt-out bits of protocol circuitry, a task which even an advanced AI engineer would have dismissed as impossible.

See-Threepio was now fully conscious, even if his outer covering was lacking—Anakin was only able to find metal plating for the torso, and the arms and legs were still bound-together bundles of wires and cables. Despite this shortcoming, Threepio accompanied his master to a Jawa barter meet on behalf of Watto. The droid's fluency with languages helped Anakin hammer out a fair price for the merchandise and came in handy when they ran across a wounded Tusken Raider on the way home. Several days later, in Anakin's room, See-Threepio met Padmé Naberrie of Naboo and another droid who would be a familiar presence in the years to come—a squat little astromech model with the unit designation R2-D2.

Threepio and Artoo-Detoo spent long hours together helping Master Anakin prepare his Podracer for the upcoming championships. Despite their obvious differences, they quickly developed a comfortable working relationship. But when Master Anakin unexpectedly won the race—winning his freedom in the process—he departed Tatooine in the company of Artoo, Padmé, and two Jedi Knights. Threepio was left behind in the squalid Mos Espa slave quarters with Anakin's mother, Shmi.

Over the years Threepio ventured out into the galaxy and drifted through a variety of jobs, including programming converters and binary load lifters. He once spent a month running a shovel loader, and on another occasion was the personal caregiver for a Hutt child. Eventually, he and Artoo crossed paths again, and the two seemingly mismatched droids became an inseparable pair.

At one point, more than two standard decades after Threepio's creation, the two droids were won by a smuggler in a gambling match. Their newest master had only owned them for a few days when his ship was intercepted by police vessels above Ingo. To save his skin, the smuggler dumped his contraband cargo—including the droids—and fled. A pair of young humans, Jord Dusat and Thall Joben, salvaged Artoo and Threepio. Their new masters led them to the neighboring planet Annoo and got them embroiled in a scheme to hijack the weapons satellite *Trigon One*. A visit to the famed Boonta speeder races followed, and a breezy hotrod rally turned into a life-or-death struggle with the bounty hunter Boba Fett. Master Thall was eventually offered a job with Zebulon Dak Speeders, a corporation run by an eccentric engineer who disliked droids to the point of paranoia. In order to ensure their master's bright future, Artoo and Threepio voluntarily resigned their employment.

Intergalactic Droid Agency picked them up next. This regional company operated a stable of droids that they hired out on temporary assignments. Artoo and Threepio were sent to the Doodnik Café on the mining planet Tyne's Horky. There, they proved to be the worst waiters the locals had ever seen. Both droids were soon purchased in an auction by Jann Tosh.

Master Jann took them to Tammuz-an, where they helped the planetary monarch Mon Julpa win back his rightful throne. In gratitude, Mon Julpa gave Jann a piloting job flying escort for the Tammuz-an shipping fleet. Julpa's starfighters were state-of-the-art R-22 Spearheads—a design later copied by the Rebel Alliance when they developed the A-wing fighter—and the agile vessels were instrumental in the defeat of the Tarnoonga pirates. The droids even helped cripple the Tarnoonga pirate ship, a modified Imperial Star Destroyer dubbed *Demolisher*.

Master Jann released Artoo-Detoo and See-Threepio from his service when he enrolled in the Imperial Academy at Raithal. On his way coreward, Jann dropped the droids off on Manda, a crossroads planet where he was scheduled to catch a commercial starliner. The droids remained on Manda for weeks, scrubbing down the saltwater tanks in the starport hotel after the aquatic guests checked out each morning. Eventually they were purchased by a guest, Mungo Baobab, the wealthy heir to the Baobab Merchant Fleet. Master Mungo took his new droids with him to Roon, where they participated in the Roon Colonial Games and defeated the evil Governor Koong of Tawntoom province. Though Mungo's quest to discover a commercially exploitable supply of priceless Roonstone gems failed, he salvaged enough Roonstones to make his adventure profitable.

Mungo Baobab proved to be a kindly master, and the droids continued in his service as he grew the Baobab Merchant Fleet and established a lucrative three-point trade route between Roon, Manda, and Ryloth. Threepio used his skill with ancient languages to help Mungo translate *Dha Werda Verda,* an epic poem etched into the crystalline structure of several of the recovered Roonstones. These unexpected ancient inscriptions were intriguing. Master Mungo sent Threepio to the Baobab Archives to translate the rest of the engravings, but the two droids arrived at their destination without an electronic confirmation of their orders. The researchers already had plenty of Telbrintel science droids assigned to the task and didn't need a protocol unit, and they certainly didn't require the services of a mere astromech. Despite Threepio's indignant protests that they be allowed to contact Master Mungo at once, the two companions were sold to a trafficker in used technological goods.

A string of unremarkable and menial assignments ended when Threepio and Artoo were purchased by Governor Wena, a panjandrum representing the Kalarba system. Wena served Kalarba as a roving ambassador, flitting from system to system in an opulent diplomatic starship. His tastes were indulgent and his expense reports outrageous. Every droid on his luxurious vessel was retuned, recalibrated, and lavishly oiled at least once per day. Threepio never wanted to leave. Even Artoo, who had little to do in the fully automated environment, enjoyed the extravagance. Soon, however, news of Wena's excesses reached his superiors on Kalarba. Funds were cut off and he was ordered to repay millions of credits for "unnecessary expenses." Wena was forced to place most of his possessions on the auction block. A junk trader purchased See-Threepio and Artoo-Detoo at rock-bottom prices. Ironically, they were placed on a barge bound for the Kalarba system, home of the now ex-Governor Wena.

The barge arrived at Hosk Station, a city-covered moon orbiting Kalarba. One of the many passengers aboard the passage boat was an assassin droid—one of the four IG-88 units from Halowan Labs. IG-88 escaped, throwing Hosk Station into a panic. During the confusion the droids boarded a ship and ejected its lifepod onto the surface of Kalarba. Fortuitously, they were immediately taken in by the wealthy Pitareeze family, owners of the patent on the legendary Pitareeze MT-5 hyperdrive unit. Threepio cared for the Pitareeze boy, Nak, and Artoo became an accomplished chef onboard the Pitareeze family tour ship, inventing a tasty recipe for Stenness pie. During a day trip to Hosk Station, Threepio was mistaken for the assassin droid C-3PX and nearly dismantled in a no-holds-barred death match in Hosk Arena. On another visit to Hosk, the droids prevented the terminal's main power core from overloading. In gratitude, they were both deputized by Unit Zed, Chief of Hosk

111010000011110010100011101
1001010010100100010010100010011001011001000

111010000011110010100011101101101111011010101010101001001010101101101001000010101001010100101001010010101

Robotic Security, and authorized to hunt down the fugitive outlaw Olag Greck. Baron Pitareeze gave the mission his blessing, and the droids left aboard Unit Zed's police ship.

Greck's trail led to the notorious Smuggler's Moon of Nar Shaddaa. Unit Zed, a police droid, was authorized to operate autonomously, but the slum dwellers of Nar Shaddaa had no respect for law officers, robotic or otherwise. Unit Zed was blasted to scrap and See-Threepio lost his left leg below the knee. A mysterious droid named B-9D7 became Threepio's benefactor, replacing his missing limb with a new silver leg, but this foreign hardware was a curse, not a gift. A hidden programming module superimposed a confident, heroic personality over Threepio's fainthearted and fearful one and caused the droid to incite a robotic revolution against the droid manufacturer Boonda the Hutt. The revolution came to a quick end when it was discovered that B-9D7, actually the human industrialist Movo Brattakin in the body of a droid, had orchestrated the events to eliminate his business rival Boonda. When a sleeper bomb was discovered inside Threepio's leg, the offending limb was replaced with a golden spare and the droid's original personality programming was restored.

The droids returned to Nar Shaddaa after their adventure, but Threepio had no desire to spend any more time on the Smuggler's Moon. An Ithorian botanist named Zorneth soon hired both droids to assist him on his starship, a *Shamarok*-class herdship containing a greenhouse and a menagerie. Master Zorneth was a distant sort, driven by his innate pacifism and his obsession with the genetically engineered herb savorium. The potent seasoning, developed five years earlier by botanist Klorr Vilia, eliminated the brain's capacity for negative emotions and produced mindless, happy buffoons nicknamed "smilers." Dictator-Forever Craw, undisputed ruler of Targonn in the

0011101000001111002010001110

010001010010101001001001001010101000100101111010101010100100011100101010010100010100100100010101010001001110

Periphery region, stole both Artoo and Threepio in an attempt to learn the secret of the savorium herb. A band of Targonnian revolutionaries helped the droids escape and return to Master Zorneth, but the herdship's supply of savorium was destroyed to prevent it from falling into Craw's talons. As the herdship burst into flames, the droids obeyed Zorneth's final order and escaped in a lifepod.

Unfortunately the tiny vessel lacked a hyperdrive. At maximum sublight speed it took two months of travel—and a lifetime's worth of bickering and banter—for the droids to reach a major shipping lane and rescue in the Tion Hegemony, a remote but historically significant corner of space. See-Threepio found it fascinating to be stationed in the old stomping grounds of Xim the Despot, and their new master seemed to be a thoughtful and eager young man. Diplomats of the Tion Hegemony, Jake Harthan and his father were attempting to establish a trade route with the planet Tahlboor, which was embroiled in an ancient feud of blood hatred. During negotiations, See-Threepio was purchased by one faction and Artoo by the other, giving them a unique vantage point on the monumental events that unfolded. Thanks to the droids' detective work, a traitor was exposed and the Tahlboor civil war reached a temporary cease-fire. The droids ended their adventure as the property of Larka, a young Tahlboorian woman who wished to see the stars.

Mistress Larka gave way to other masters and mistresses, but eventually both droids found lasting employment with the Royal House of Alderaan. After years of rudderless drifting, See-Threepio finally felt he had come into his own. Threepio was kept busy with political formalities and, except for a frustrating year spent in the palace preschool, he couldn't have been happier. It was a rude shock, then, when he was assigned to the consular ship *Tantive IV* and demoted to the labor pool. Even though the assignment was temporary—one interpreter per astromech for the duration of the voyage—Threepio couldn't help but feel resentful towards all astromechs for *requiring* translators in the first place. And of course, his astromech partner *would* have to be a certain familiar little troublemaker . . . .

See-Threepio and Artoo-Detoo were soon called out of the labor pool on a special assignment for the ship's captain, Colton Antilles, for whom Threepio had worked as a translator. Captain Antilles and Her Royal Highness Leia Organa were waiting for the droids in the bridge. For security purposes, the captain issued the voice override code Epsilon Actual, ordering both droids to restrict and protect Leia Organa's presence aboard the *Tantive IV* at all costs.

On the Princess' orders, Artoo-Detoo passed through the bridge airlock and jetted to the *Tantive IV*'s navi-computer sensor suite. There, the astromech droid pretended to make extravehicular repairs. The Princess commented that the ruse might help explain their presence in the restricted Toprawa system, but the Imperial Star Destroyer *Devastator* was obviously unconvinced. As the *Devastator* closed to firing range, Princess Leia reported that an incoming data stream from Toprawa's surface had completed transmission. The *Tantive IV* powered up its engines for lightspeed, and Artoo-Detoo ducked back inside the ship at the last possible instant. Captain Antilles instructed both droids to return to their previous duties.

Threepio circumspectly took what he termed "the long way" on his return from the *Tantive IV*'s bridge. After all, while Captain Antilles had ordered them to return to the labor pool, he hadn't specified a timetable. With any luck, they'd be back at Alderaan before he had to face that miserable labor pool overseer again. He and Artoo slowly shuffled from the galley to the armory to the

1101000001111001010001110110111101
100101001

0010100101010010010010010101010001001011110101010101001000111001010010100010

010101001001010101101101001000010101001010100100100111010000

engineering deck, scarcely rating a second glance from the preoccupied human crew. When the vessel reverted from hyperspace, a soft thudding came from somewhere above the droids' heads—the sound of turbolaser bolts hitting the dorsal shields.

The two droids hurried out into a corridor as Alderaanian troopers rushed to battle stations. The lights dimmed and the artificial gravity undulated as the ship suffered an exceptionally violent blast. **"Did you hear that?"** asked Threepio, detecting a dwindling mechanical rumble amid the shouts and chaos. **"They've shut down the main reactor. We'll be destroyed for sure!"** With the reactor offline, no power was available to feed the sublight engines. The ship was soon seized in a tractor beam by their unseen assailant.

The boarding party arrived in a cloud of smoke and a fusillade of laser blasts. It had been some time since Threepio had last crossed paths with Imperial stormtroopers, but their relentless aggression was all too familiar. He turned tail and fled, so concerned with his own self-preservation that he didn't immediately notice that his counterpart was no longer with him. **"Artoo-Detoo, where are you?"** he wailed. At last he rounded a corner and spotted his friend—and a human figure? he couldn't be sure—at the far end of a maintenance alcove. **"What are we going to do?"** Threepio blurted as he clattered forward. The ghostly white figure he thought he'd seen a moment earlier had vanished. **"We'll be sent to the spice mines of Kessel or smashed into who knows what!"**

Artoo-Detoo rolled past his friend at top speed without a single sympathetic beep. Threepio followed him due aft, quickly arriving at the ship's stern bank of emergency lifepods. **"You're not allowed in there,"** Threepio pointed out primly. **"It's restricted. You'll be deactivated for sure."** Artoo's reply was appallingly ill-mannered, even for him. **"Don't call me a mindless philosopher, you**

overweight glob of grease!" Threepio shot back in kind. Artoo twittered out a harried explanation as he fiddled with the manual release for the pod's entry hatch. *Plans? A secret mission? A
nearby explosion brought an end to further discussion and both droids scrambled inside. The
pod's holding clamps retracted with a clang, and the lifeboat lurched sickeningly as it dropped
away from the *Tantive IV* in free fall.

Artoo tapped at the pod's simple controls with his manipulator arm, firing the steering
thrusters in short controlled bursts. The pod rolled and Threepio caught a glimpse of the yellow
disk far below them. This certainly wasn't Alderaan, or even another world in its star system. As
they plummeted through the atmosphere, Artoo activated the pod's meager braking jets, which
proved insufficient to prevent a gyro-rattling impact into the planet's surface. Both droids bounced
off all four walls of the cramped cabin. See-Threepio popped the hatch and poked his head out, taking in the dismal surroundings with a panoramic sensor scan. Sand. Endless sand.

Grumbling to himself, Threepio helped Artoo out of the beached pod. The ungrateful little astromech immediately set off across the desert. Threepio hurried to catch up, irked at being
ignored and convinced that, by the sheer virtue of his superior processing power, he should be the
one to lead this spur-of-the-moment expedition. Artoo tootled and made a hard turn to the right.
"Wait a minute. Where do you think you're going?" said Threepio. **"Well, I'm not going that way,"**
he declared. **"It's much too rocky. This way is much easier."** Artoo blatted a stubborn reply, once
again mentioning his "secret mission." Threepio was fed up. **"I've just about had enough of you,"** he
huffed. **"Go that way! You'll be malfunctioning within a day, you nearsighted scrap pile."** He punc-
tuated his words with a sharp kick. **"And don't let me catch you following me, begging for help,**

0001001010100101110110010101011010010010010010010000100111101010101010100100101010011000111010011101000001111001010100011101

46

C-3PO: TALES OF THE GOLDEN DROID

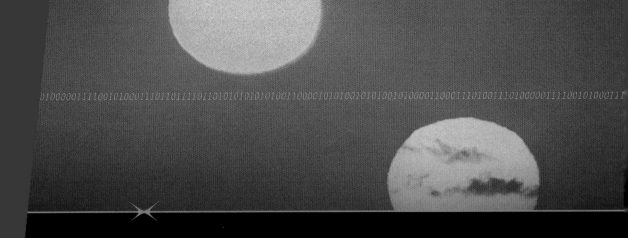

because you won't get it." Threepio marched resolutely in the opposite direction, burying his hurt feelings beneath his wounded pride.

The unforgiving heat and punishing radiation from the planet's double suns grew even more intense as the twins rose towards the sky's zenith. Sandwhirls, kicked up by unpredictable eddies of wind, drove silica and flecks of grit deep into Threepio's powerbus cables and oil tubes. After hours of marching he had crossed uncounted kilometers, and still the horizon showed no sign of change. **"That malfunctioning little twerp!"** he fumed. **"He tricked me into going this way! But he'll do no better."** The forlorn droid continued his trek, passing time by running through his internal workings and cataloging the cascading systems failures. He spotted a building in the distance, though upon closer look it proved to be the bleached and desiccated skeleton of some colossal beast. A bleaker omen could scarcely be imagined.

See-Threepio scanned the horizon behind him, half hoping that Artoo might be following in his tracks. The astromech was nowhere in sight, but a huge vehicle glinted in the sunlight as it crested a distant dune. A surge of hope re-energized Threepio's circuits. **"Over here!"** he shouted, waving his arms. **"Help, please, help!"** The vehicle altered its course and ground ponderously across the sand towards Threepio. It shuddered to a halt meters away, extending a ramp from a hatchway between its colossal tank treads.

Clambering down the ramp came a horde of short, smelly, and highly animated creatures. Threepio recognized them as Jawas. Blazing yellow eyes glowed from the dark recesses of their hoods as thcy pointed at him and jabbered in a nonsensical argot. Threepio could speak Jawa, but this tribe's dialect was peppered with colloquial jargon and traders' slang. Slightly optimistic now, Threepio asked

the aliens if they had encountered another droid, a blue-and-white model about half his height, traveling over the rocks and canyons. They hadn't, but seemed unusually excited by his question. The lead Jawa leveled an ionization blaster at Threepio, and the other members of his gang fitted their new droid with an electronic restraining bolt. Threepio was roughly forced into position beneath a magnetic suction tube. Moments later he was sucked into the bowels of the massive machine.

It was a rude landing. See-Threepio delicately wobbled to his feet, pushing aside sun-cracked plasteel tubing and rusted bits of scrap metal. He was in a large, dimly lit storage hold. As his photoreceptors adjusted to the gloom he could make out dozens of other droids sitting silently among the trash: a Treadwell, an R5 unit, an EG-6 power droid—all menial brutes. An RA-7 Servant stood perched against the wall. Was that a CZ secretary droid? The CZ series was quite capable of holding a civilized conversation. He started to pick his way across the hold and suddenly stopped dead in his tracks, aghast. The Jawas had torn the poor CZ to pieces! Threepio put his back to the wall and wondered what would become of him now.

Artoo-Detoo was the next droid to arrive through the suction tube. Threepio was so overjoyed to see a familiar face he forgot their earlier disagreement. Artoo huffily reminded him and accused his friend, correctly, of directing the scavenging aliens right to him. In spite of it all each droid was glad to find the other safe and sound. The strange salvage vehicle rumbled on interminably. No sense of day or night penetrated the hull, and Threepio was no longer sure of the accuracy of his internal chronometer. At last, the constant jouncing ceased and the transport ground to a halt. Chattering Jawas ratcheted open the cargo door, spilling harsh morning light into the chamber.

10000110001110100111010000011110001000111011011110110101010101010100110000101010011

THE SAGA OF SEE-THREEPIO

It wasn't the first time the two companions had been up for auction. Obediently, Artoo and Threepio filed out of the vehicle to stand at attention on the hardpacked sand of a hardscrabble moisture farm. A roughly built human regarded Threepio with a practiced eye. "You!" he barked, a touch of amusement in his voice. "I suppose you're programmed for etiquette and protocol." **"Protocol! Why it's my primary function, sir. I am well versed in all the custom . . ."** The tactic failed, and Threepio silently berated himself for his short-sightedness; farms need laborers, not consular attachés! **"Sir, my first job was programming binary load lifters, very similar to your vaporators in most respects. I am—"** The farmer interrupted the sales pitch by asking him if he could speak the Bocce dialect. The man actually needed a linguist! **"Of course I can, sir,"** he babbled. **"It's like a second language to me. I am—"** The man gruffly ordered him to shut up, then informed the Jawas that he'd be purchasing the protocol unit. See-Threepio was overwhelmed with happiness and relief. **"Shutting up, sir,"** he reported dutifully.

He'd done it! Triumphantly, he stepped out of line and stood next to another human in a dirty white tunic. But when he turned back to regard the losers' row, his spirits sank. Artoo's unblinking radar eye gazed forlornly back at him as a red R5 unit extended its third tread and wheeled slowly towards the farm. Threepio wavered, at a loss for what to do. Salvation was so close, but if he and Artoo parted company here they might never cross paths again. Curse the little greasepot for putting him into this position, anyhow!

Pop! The red R5 unit blew its stack in spectacular fashion, scattering motivator components across the desert floor amid a belch of oily smoke. Threepio silently thanked the Maker and tapped his new owner on the shoulder. **"Excuse me, sir,"** he began, pointing one servogrip in Artoo's

direction, **"but that R2 unit is in prime condition. A real bargain."** The Jawas reluctantly accepted the swap, and Artoo joined his old friend as the human headed for the rounded bulges of the underground homestead. **"Now don't you forget this,"** nagged Threepio. **"Why I should stick my neck out for you is quite beyond my capacity."**

They stepped out of the sunlight into a cluttered tech dome that smelled of rags and oil. A T-16 Skyhopper, one stabilizer twisted out of shape, rested in an adjacent hangar. The young man hooked Artoo to a power generator and guided Threepio onto a lift platform that descended into a voluminous oil bath. Things were definitely looking up.

Their new master introduced himself as Luke. He seemed frustrated and was clearly hoping to be somewhere else. Threepio's offer to help was rebuffed, but in a gentle tone. Master Luke scraped at Artoo's chassis with a chrome pick. As he turned his head to ask another question, the fragment he was picking at abruptly snapped in two, propelling Luke backwards onto the garage floor with a grunt. Simultaneously, Artoo's holoprojector flickered to life and projected a ghostly blue image of Princess Leia Organa. Threepio recognized her instantly, but he was physically incapable of ignoring Captain Antilles' Epsilon Actual command: restrict and protect all references to Leia Organa's presence aboard the *Tantive IV*. "Who is she?" Master Luke demanded. "She's beautiful." Threepio tried his best to avoid an outright lie. **"I think she was a passenger on our last voyage. A person of some importance, I believe."**

Artoo whistled out a communication for his counterpart to translate and Threepio paused, baffled. Now *this* was something he didn't recognize at all. **"He says he's the property of Obi-Wan Kenobi,"** he finally managed. **"And it's a private message for him. Quite frankly, I don't know what**

he's talking about." Oddly, Master Luke seemed familiar with the name, and was eager to see more of the droid's recording. When Artoo explained that the restraining bolt had caused a short in his holorecorder, Luke popped the bolt loose. The hologram vanished.

Luke protested loudly and Artoo squeaked a meek reply, one that Threepio was too mortified to translate. "**What message?!**" His hand clonked loudly on Artoo's head dome. "**The one you've just been playing! The one you're carrying inside your rusty innards!**" Threepio apologized as their new master left the tech dome, leaving the two droids alone together. Threepio was furious. Yet another promising situation sabotaged by that anarchist's idea of a joke. "**I don't think he likes you at all,**" he said. Artoo whistled a melancholy interrogative. "**No,**" Threepio replied frostily. "**I don't like you either.**"

Threepio was in no mood for further discussion but Artoo persisted. The little droid revealed that his holographic imaging system was fully operational. He had reported the short circuit in order to rid himself of the restraining bolt. Threepio listened in horror as the plucky astromech announced his intention to set off that instant across the trackless wastes in search of Obi-Wan Kenobi. Threepio's pleas—droids simply didn't *do* these things—fell on deaf audio pickups. Artoo could not ignore his "mission," even if it meant leaving his oldest friend behind. With a beep of sadness, Artoo-Detoo rolled out of the tech dome.

At first, Threepio was enraged. Deserted! After he'd gone out on a limb to rescue the rotten, cut-rate little ingrate from the droid auction! What would Master Luke do when he discovered what had happened? It was the scrap heap for sure, or at the very least a memory wipe. Suddenly panicked, Threepio hid behind the family four-seat landspeeder and hoped for a miracle.

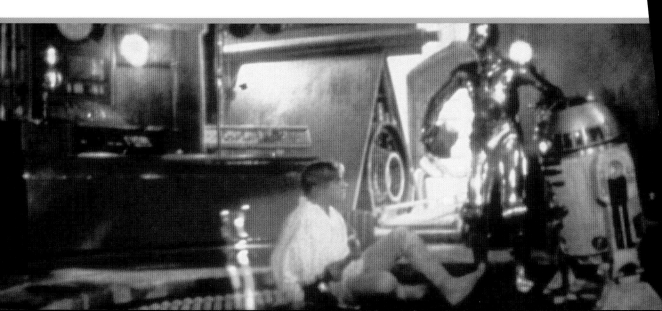

11010100101001010100100101001010010010010010100100

C-3PO: TALES OF THE GOLDEN DROID

The restraining bolt sent a jolt of electricity coursing through every circuit, and with a spastic jerk Threepio came to full wakefulness. Master Luke stood in the now-darkened tech dome, finger depressed on the button of his droid caller. **"It wasn't my fault, sir! Please don't deactivate me!"** Luke sprinted outside to scan through a pair of long-range macrobinoculars, but a full sweep turned up no sign of the runaway droid. Master Luke was distressed, but not furious. "You know, that little droid is going to cause me a lot of trouble," he remarked. Threepio couldn't agree more.

At the break of dawn, Luke and Threepio went in search of their wayward droid. Threepio took the speeder's controls as Luke worked the vehicle's primitive scanning equipment. Before long they had located their fugitive. **"Master Luke here is your rightful owner,"** lectured Threepio, who felt no small measure of relief despite his obvious irritation. **"You're fortunate he doesn't blast you into a million pieces right here!"** Artoo acted sheepish but suddenly let loose a frantic flurry of whistles. Threepio translated the news of mysterious lifeforms closing in on their position. "Come on," Master Luke called. "Let's have a look."

With difficulty, Threepio scaled the incline. Master Luke lay flat on the stone, peering through his macrobinoculars. Without warning a masked Tusken Raider sprang up from behind the ridge, howling and wielding a metal axe. The savage barbarian took a vigorous swing at Threepio's midsection, sending the golden droid tumbling down the rocky slope. The banging rattled his cognitive circuitry so badly he slipped into shutdown, and the last thing he saw through his bumping, bouncing vision was a very large rock. When Master Luke hit his reactivate switch, he discovered his restraining bolt had popped free and his left arm had been torn loose at the shoulder. **"You go on without**

101001000010101001010100101001010101
111010100100011110110101010111100101010101101101001000010101001010100010

me, Master Luke," he said bravely. "**I'm done for!**"

Luke would have none of it, and the group took the landspeeder to the desert hermitage of a new arrival, Ben Kenobi. Inside, Luke borrowed the old man's tools and expertly reconnected the automatic linkages in Threepio's arm. Grateful for the help and relieved that the damage appeared to be minimal, Threepio asked permission to close down his primary systems in order to run an internal diagnostic program. Luke agreed, and Threepio retreated to an inner world of recharge patterns and circuit schematics.

When he awoke, the group was preparing to leave. Master Luke had agreed to take his elderly rescuer—the Clone Wars hero and Republic General Obi-Wan Kenobi, according to Artoo—to the nearby city of Anchorhead. During the journey they spotted a plume of black smoke that proved to mark the death of a Jawa sandcrawler. While Master Luke raced home to discover the tragic fate of his childhood guardians, Threepio and Artoo helped General Kenobi construct a burning pyre for the corpses of the murdered Jawa scavengers.

Eventually the group arrived at the spaceport-city of Mos Eisley. Droids, pedestrians, and towering saurian creatures clogged the thoroughfares, and the sky was dark with arriving and departing space traffic. It wasn't until they had descended into the smoke-filled darkness of a squalid star-pilot cantina that they attracted any attention. "Hey!" shouted the bartender, thrusting a meaty hand in the direction of Luke's two automated companions. "We don't serve their kind here." Like most long-lived mechanicals, See-Threepio was well acquainted with anti-droid prejudice and the people who practiced it. When Master Luke suggested they return to the landspeeder for their own safety he could hardly disagree.

From their new vantage point Artoo and Threepio noticed several stormtrooper squads

gearing up for a search. Threepio briefly considered warning Master Luke, but decided that such an action would only draw attention. He and Artoo avoided the Imperial sweep by blending in with the display stock on a used-droid lot, and then reconnected with Luke and Obi-Wan at the speeder. The humans needed to sell their vehicle to raise capital, so Luke ordered the droids to head for Docking Bay 94. On the way, they ran across another stormtrooper patrol and bluffed their way into a local domicile by posing as representatives from the Skywalker Technical Maintenance Service. Threepio locked the door and waited until the danger was long past before poking his head out. **"I don't know what all this trouble is about,"** he griped, **"but I'm sure it must be your fault."** Artoo's retort was scandalously vulgar. **"You watch your language!"**

Master Luke and General Kenobi rendezvoused with the droids near Docking Bay 94 and the quartet descended the stairs. The general had booked passage on a dilapidated-looking light freighter with the incongruously dashing moniker *Millennium Falcon*. The ship's captain, a lanky Corellian named Han Solo, and the first mate, a ferocious Wookiee named Chewbacca, waited uneasily near the boarding ramp. Threepio strapped himself into an acceleration couch in the forward hold and the freighter roared off amid a hail of stormtrooper laser fire. **"Oh, my,"** he moaned. **"I'd forgotten how much I hate space travel."**

As soon as the *Falcon* made the transition to the smoothness of hyperspace, the passengers relaxed and settled into the routine pastimes of a space voyage. With Threepio as his unbidden coach, Artoo challenged Chewbacca to a friendly match of dejarik holo-chess. When the Wookiee reacted badly to a well-played capture, Captain Solo warned them not to anger his copilot. **"But sir,"** Threepio protested, **"nobody worries about upsetting a droid."** Solo rolled his eyes. "That's 'cause droids don't pull

people's arms out of their sockets when they lose," he explained with a self-confident smirk. Threepio looked at the hairy, muscular beast and had no doubt he could do exactly that. **"I suggest a new strategy, Artoo,"** he counseled. **"Let the Wookiee win."**

A proximity alarm pinged on the technical station, indicating imminent reversion to realspace. Captain Solo and Chewbacca charged up the connection hallway into the cockpit with Obi-Wan and Luke not far behind, leaving the droids alone in the forward hold. Threepio settled back in the acceleration couch and allowed himself to revel in his imminent return to Alderaan. Before the night was through he could be attending a reception banquet for General Kenobi or assisting Bail Organa's staff in greeting the new ambassadorial corps! A sudden jolt shook the *Falcon* from stem to stern and nearly threw Threepio to the deck. An intense whine, steadily building in pitch, came from somewhere behind the aft cargo hold; Artoo warbled that the auxiliary power reserves had been dumped into the sublight engine bank, and the system would have to be shut down immediately to avoid a burnout. On cue, the engines stuttered down to idle and three humans and a Wookiee burst back into the hold, all shouts and noise and chaos.

Master Luke hurriedly explained that they had *not* arrived at Alderaan. Indeed, there was no longer any Alderaan for them to arrive at. Threepio heard more shouts, frantic orders, and something about a moon-sized battle station. The next thing he knew, Captain Solo was ordering everyone into a long, narrow compartment hidden beneath the walkway deckplates.

See-Threepio switched the wavelength of his photoreceptors from the visible to the infrared spectrum. The three humans sat crouched at the opposite end, heads cocked oddly towards the ceiling to pick up audio signals in the absence of sight. There was a gentle thud as the *Falcon* touched

110010101010100101010101010101010101010100001011111010000101010010100111110010101010010101
1010101010001010

down. Minutes later, the sharp staccato of armored boots echoed above their heads, then faded. Captain Solo popped the upper deckplate, allowing light and cool recycled air to wash into the chamber.

It was a foolhardy plan. The heart of an Imperial battle station would undoubtedly be swarming with stormtroopers. Threepio wondered why no one else was able to see the wisdom of a tactical surrender. When a pair of Imperial scanning technicians ascended the ramp, Chewbacca knocked them senseless. The two stormtroopers that followed were stunned with a blaster shot. Before he knew it, Threepio was following the disguised Captain Solo out of the ship and up the lift platform to the hangar control booth. After a quick shootout the group had the space all to themselves.

Threepio and Artoo obeyed General Kenobi's instructions to locate the mainframe terminal. Like most Imperial computer banks, the docking bay gantry controls had a scomp-link interface port conveniently located at the height of an R2 astromech droid. **"We've found the computer outlet, sir,"** Threepio reported. Artoo's data-link arm nestled into the socket. In seconds, he located the couplings that powered the tractor beam, and Obi-Wan departed alone.

Artoo's excited bleeps surprised the room, and Threepio did his best to keep up with the stream of information spat out by his overexcited friend. **"I'm afraid I'm not quite sure, sir,"** he explained apologetically. **"He says, 'I found her' and keeps repeating, 'she's here.'"** Further questioning revealed that the Princess Leia Organa was a prisoner aboard this very battle station. **"I'm afraid she's scheduled to be terminated."**

Master Luke convinced his two mercenary companions to throw together a rescue opera-

1001010101010101
1011111010000101010010100111110010101011010101010001010100010

C-3PO: TALES OF THE GOLDEN DROID

tion. For a terrifying moment Threepio thought he and Artoo would be compelled to join the trio in mass suicide, but his master was content to leave them behind in the control tower. Alone. **"Master Luke, sir,"** he piped up. **"Pardon me for asking . . . but, ah . . . what should Artoo and I do if we're discovered here?"** Luke shrugged and suggested they simply keep the door locked. Captain Solo joined in with a leer, clearly enjoying the golden droid's discomfort. "And hope they don't have blasters," he added. Miffed, Threepio dropped one metal arm on his companion's head dome with a soft clack. **"That isn't very reassuring."**

The moment the would-be rescuers left the room, Threepio activated the interior lockout. Now there was little to do but wait for the return of Master Luke or General Kenobi. Artoo trundled back over to the computer access port and plugged in, sifting through the multiple data layers to determine if the progress of the humans had been unnoticed. For a time, all was quiet. Then a warning alarm shrieked and the console threat board lit up like a pyrotechnics display.

Artoo reported the bleak news: The central security garrison had posted a station-wide alert regarding a botched rescue on Level 5. Threepio fretted while Artoo called up a schematic of the cell bay in the hopes he could lend a remote assist. Abruptly, Threepio's handheld comlink crackled to life with Master Luke's desperate calls. The rescuers were trapped like vrelts in a well. **"All systems have been alerted to your presence, sir,"** Threepio explained. **"The main entrance seems to be the only way out."** Artoo's whistles were interrupted by a sharp rapping on the outer door. "Open up in there!" came an authoritative voice. **"Oh, no,"** Threepio managed, letting the comlink fall from his metal fingers as his servos momentarily seized up in terror.

Artoo-Detoo kept a level head. Scooting over to the storage locker on the side wall, he

keyed open the door and blatted for Threepio to join him inside. Threepio tottered over to the closet, sealing the door moments before the stormtrooper squad blasted through the outer lock. Threepio did his best to collect his racing thoughts, and when the the closet door opened, he launched into a terrified act that was not hard to fake. **"They're madmen!"** he blurted, staring down the shiny black barrels of two stormtrooper rifles. Knowing that the prison breakout had been broadcast throughout the entire station, Threepio continued, **"They're heading for the prison level. If you hurry, you might catch them!"** The trooper commander departed down the hallway, taking four of his men with him.

Obviously, the room had been compromised, and neither Master Luke nor General Kenobi would be able to return there. See-Threepio retrieved the comlink he'd dropped and headed for the door, where he was surprised by a remaining stormtrooper sentry. **"All this excitement has overrun the circuits in my counterpart here,"** Threepio bluffed, thinking fast. **"If you don't mind, I'd like to take him down to maintenance."** The guard nodded and the two passed into the corridor beyond.

They went down one level to the main forward bay. **"They aren't here!"** Threepio fretted. **"See if they've been captured."** Artoo plugged into another wall socket and learned that the alert status was unchanged. He twisted his head dome and warbled a shrill reminder. **"Use the comlink?"** repeated Threepio. **"Oh my! I forgot, I turned it off."** Threepio reactivated the unit and heard Master Luke's pained voice shouting for Artoo to cut the power to all the detention level garbage mashers.

Garbage mashers! Suddenly realizing what could befall his master, Threepio frantically relayed the command to his counterpart. Artoo furiously manipulated the Imperial data network, but

only hysterical screams came through the comlink. **"Curse my metal body, I wasn't fast enough!"** Threepio cried out, grief-stricken. **"It's all my fault!"** Master Luke soon set him straight, and told the two life-saving droids to wait for them by the ship.

Armed stormtroopers were stationed on the floor of the docking bay. The droids hid behind a pile of storage canisters, and when the sentries wandered off to investigate a stir near the hangar doors, Threepio took command. **"Come on, Artoo, we're going."** The droids boarded the *Falcon* and the others soon followed, including the Princess, who recognized Threepio and Artoo from the *Tantive IV*. Sadly, General Kenobi had been killed on board the battle station. A quartet of TIE fighters tried to prevent their escape to hyperspace, but the sturdy Corellian freighter survived with only minor damage. The remainder of their trip to the remote planet Yavin was blissfully uneventful.

The *Millennium Falcon* skimmed low over Yavin's fourth moon, a lush, verdant orb dotted with the crumbling stone ziggurats of an extinct alien species. A Rebel flight crewman guided the freighter to a landing spot inside the Rebel Alliance's hidden base. The Rebel leaders greeted Princess Leia warmly, and whisked Artoo-Detoo to the computer center. See-Threepio watched as Rebel technicians and slicer droids downloaded a voluminous amount of data. An advanced decryption algorithm quickly decoded the files, revealing the technical schematics for an Imperial battle station, the aptly named Death Star.

Although it felt good to be surrounded by senators, generals, commanders, and administrative staffers, Threepio knew the greatest danger was yet to come. Qualified pilots were desperately needed to go up against the oncoming Death Star, and the Alliance's X-wing and Y-wing fighters

required astromech droids as plug-in counterparts. Master Luke and Artoo-Detoo volunteered. Threepio ventured into the flight hangar and watched apprehensively as Artoo was lowered into position in the fuselage of Luke's X-wing. **"You've got to come back,"** he pleaded. **"You wouldn't want my life to get boring, would you?"** He couldn't bear to watch the fighters depart. Princess Leia kindly invited him into the operations center to observe the Rebellion's last stand.

Threepio wasn't skilled in interpreting the battle data displayed on the table-sized tactical unit, but he listened intently for any news concerning X-wing Red Five. The Rebels' first trench run failed miserably, their second fared no better. Red dots representing Alliance starfighters winked off the display at an alarming rate. Finally, Master Luke took the point in a last-ditch attempt at running the trench. On the display, three green Imperial icons zeroed in on Red Five, and Luke's escorts were quickly chased off or eliminated. And then came the words Threepio feared most of all—*I've lost Artoo.*

Moments later, the Death Star was reported destroyed. The control room erupted in unrestrained jubilation, but Threepio wanted no part of the gaiety. *I've lost Artoo*—what could Master Luke mean? Frantic with worry, on the brink of despair, Threepio made his way back down to the flight hangar.

The ground crew was lowering Artoo-Detoo from the battle-scarred X-wing when he arrived. Judging by the extent of the damage, Artoo appeared to have taken a cannon blast square in the center of his head dome. Threepio pushed through the crowd to his friend's side. The poor, brave little fool! **"You can repair him, can't you?"** Threepio inquired of the head mechanic. **"You _must_ repair him. Sir, if any of my circuits or gears will help, I'll gladly donate them."** Artoo-Detoo was wheeled

C-3PO: Tales of the Golden Droid

away to the cybernetic equivalent of an intensive-care trauma center. "He'll be all right," assured Master Luke.

The Grand Reception Hall was packed with Rebel pilots, troops, and techs, dressed in uniform and assembled in orderly rows. Princess Leia stood at the front of the assemblage, radiant in her senatorial gown and glittering Organa royal jewelry. Luke Skywalker and Han Solo strode confidently up the center aisle to receive heavy golden medallions and accept the highest honor the Rebel Alliance could bestow. Chewbacca was also lauded. At See-Threepio's side, a fully repaired Artoo-Detoo twittered joyfully and rocked back and forth with excitement.

Immediately after the ceremony, the Rebel Alliance began preparations for the evacuation of Yavin 4 and the establishment of a new base on some lesser-known world. Many of the larger warships and equipment transports escaped into hyperspace, but the main Rebel command staff was trapped in the Yavin system by a blockade of Interdictor cruisers under the command of Imperial Admiral Griff. See-Threepio accompanied Master Luke on several dangerous runnings of the blockade, performing important missions on dismal planets such as Drexel and Aridus. Within a few months the last Rebels evacuated Yavin 4 just ahead of Darth Vader's command ship *Executor*.

The fleet hopped across the galaxy for a time, winning new allies to the Rebel cause and securing valuable supplies. Eventually the Rebel Alliance leadership agreed to construct a new command base and selected the planet Hoth, an ice world first encountered by Luke and Threepio in the weeks following the Battle of Yavin.

Where Tatooine was sweltering, Hoth was frost-bitten. But the two planets had more in common than Threepio liked—both were desolate wastelands with temperatures well outside his

operational safety limits. The Rebel command staff settled in the newly christened Echo Base, a warren of ice tunnels carved by the Alliance Corps of Engineers. Construction continued over the following weeks as scouts patrolled the territory on native tauntauns and Rebel techs adapted their equipment to the freezing cold.

Threepio and Artoo were assigned as personal assistants to Princess Leia Organa. Then, Artoo nearly sabotaged their comfortable station by boosting the thermal heater in the Princess' quarters. Threepio refused to share the blame, his perfectly innocent comments about the room's unpleasant temperature weren't responsible for the catastrophic melting of the ice walls.

This minor incident was quickly forgotten when Master Luke failed to return from a routine tauntaun patrol. The Princess, deeply concerned, told the droid pair to locate Captain Solo. The Corellian captain was in an even more foul mood than usual. In response to Threepio's inquiry, he clamped his hand over the droid's vocabulator slot while he interrogated the deck officer on duty. Threepio's muffled protests were scorned and Captain Solo finally released him without so much as an apology. **"Impossible man,"** Threepio grumbled privately. Artoo whistled his agreement. **"Between ourselves,"** Threepio confided, **"I think Master Luke is in considerable danger."**

Night fell on Hoth. The temperature plunged to extremes that even droids couldn't endure for long. A few hours earlier, Captain Solo had mounted a tauntaun and ridden out into the blizzard in search of Master Luke. See-Threepio fretted and paced back and forth just inside the entrance to the main hangar, while Artoo maintained a vigil out in the exposed winds. Artoo swept his lifeform scanner back and forth until ice began to form on his instrument panel. Finally, Threepio convinced his determined friend to come inside for his own safety.

C-3PO: TALES OF THE GOLDEN DROID

The impenetrable shield door started its slow rumbling descent. Chewbacca howled and Artoo beeped out a bleak calculation. Out of habit, Threepio found himself translating the astromech's speech for Princess Leia. **"Artoo says the chances of survival are seven hundred twenty-five . . . to one."** The shield door's durasteel teeth bit into the ice floor with a resounding boom. **"Actually, Artoo has been known to make mistakes,"** Threepio apologized, mortified at his breach of decorum. **"From time to time. Dear, oh, dear."**

Miraculously both heroes were rescued at dawn. Master Luke required only a quick dip in a bacta tank to be brought back to full readiness. Threepio returned to duty at the communications center, where he witnessed the discovery of a metallic trespasser speeding through the snowfields of Zone Twelve. A Rebel comm officer intercepted a transmission fragment from the intruder and broadcast it over the public intercom: **"Sir, I am fluent in over six million forms of communication,"** Threepio offered. **"This signal is not used by the Alliance. It could be an Imperial code."** After a shoot-out with an Imperial probe droid, his interpretation was proven correct. General Rieekan ordered the immediate evacuation of Echo Base.

Artoo-Detoo was needed to help pilot Luke Skywalker's X-wing, which meant the two droids would once again be separated. Master Luke told Threepio to remain behind with Princess Leia and serve her in any capacity. Threepio watched as Artoo was installed into the battered starfighter's astromech socket. **"Artoo, you take good care of Master Luke now, you understand? And . . ."** Threepio paused, unsure how to say what needed to be said, then pressed on anyway. **"And do take good care of yourself."** He walked away to join the Princess in the command center, muttering sorrowfully to himself. **"Oh, dear, oh, dear."**

The battle went poorly, worse than Threepio could have imagined. Rebel officers frantically consulted tactical data screens and shouted retreat orders to their troops; there was little Threepio could do except stay out of the way. As the last Rebel trenches were overrun by Imperial AT-AT walkers, Princess Leia ordered the evacuation of the command center. A blast rocked the cavern before most of the technicians could get up from their chairs, shaking loose blocks of ice from the ceiling that flattened consoles in a shower of sparks. Most of the survivors headed through the corridor for the last transport, but Princess Leia showed no signs of abandoning her post. And, despite the imminent danger of permanent shutdown, Threepio could not abandon the Princess.

Captain Solo appeared in the doorway as another cave-in loosed a torrent of ice and debris. He insisted on escorting the Princess to an evacuation transport. **"Your Highness,"** Threepio pleaded, **"we must take this last transport. It's our only hope."** Leia reluctantly agreed, but safe passage on the fleet carrier was not to be. Echo Base was crumbling around them and the path to the south slope was hopelessly blocked. Captain Solo changed course and headed back the way he'd come, brushing by Threepio without a word.

Protocol units were never designed to run sprint races. Threepio lagged dangerously behind despite his best efforts. **"Wait . . . wait for me! Stop!"** Threepio reached the hangar door just in time to see it slide shut. All his exasperation with Captain Solo was summed up in that single gesture. **"How typical!"** he sniffed, but the door suddenly reopened and Han yanked him roughly inside. Chewbacca waited anxiously at the base of the *Millennium Falcon*'s boarding ramp and Threepio was the last one to clatter on board. He took his customary seat near the gameboard, but something on the tech station

brought him up short. Fearing the worst, he tapped in a diagnostic command which confirmed what his photoreceptors were telling him. He hurried up the cockpit tube to alert Captain Solo.

The captain was a bit preoccupied. Imperial snowtroopers were setting up a repeating blaster cannon at the far end of the hangar, and the *Falcon's* sublight engines were still offline. With mere seconds to spare, the *Millennium Falcon* blasted out of the hangar and escaped to the open space surrounding Hoth.

Captain Solo outmaneuvered three pursuing Star Destroyers, but a quartet of nimble TIE fighters proved unshakable. The only safe place within parsecs was the untraceable expanse of hyperspace. Han steadied the *Falcon's* course and prepared to make the jump to lightspeed. "Watch this!" he announced, and engaged the drive levers. Nothing happened.

"If I may say so, sir," Threepio piped up, **"I noticed earlier that the hyperdrive motivator has been damaged. It's impossible to go to lightspeed!"** Han and Chewbacca exchanged baleful looks. "We're in trouble!" Han shouted. The two pilots headed aft to improvise some on-the-fly repairs, leaving Threepio in the cockpit with the Princess. Leia did her best to lose the trailing TIEs, but she lacked the foolhardy finesse of the freighter's captain. As laser bolts splashed across the *Falcon's* shields, Threepio wailed with powerless terror. Hearing a gasp from Leia, Threepio looked up, just to see a slowly tumbling rock loom into view through the forward viewport. Leia jammed the controls hard to the left and the *Falcon* avoided a head-on collision, but the asteroid impacted solidly with the freighter's starboard particle shields. Spread out in front of them, as far as the eye could see, were more rocks. Millions more.

"Han, get up here!" Leia shouted into the intercom. Footsteps clattered up the hallway and Captain Solo vaulted into his seat. "Chewie, set 2-7-1," he ordered, announcing his intention to dive directly into the whirling maelstrom of stone. Threepio knew that organic beings sometimes indulged in unmitigated illogic, but this particular human was without a doubt the worst offender he'd ever known. **"Sir,"** he pointed out, **"the possibility of successfully navigating an asteroid field is approximately three thousand, seven hundred and twenty to one!"** The facts were ironclad, yet they meant nothing to the plainly suicidal Solo. "Never tell me the odds," the Corellian answered with a maniac's grin. The *Falcon* dipped and plunged through the asteroid storm. Threepio held his arms up over his photoreceptors, convinced that each boulder spelled an end to their lives. At last Captain Solo dove for one of the largest rocks, a small planetoid. **"Oh, this is suicide,"** Threepio moaned, but soon they entered a darkened tunnel and touched down safely and quietly.

Everyone stood and stretched, grateful for the temporary reprieve. The malfunctioning hyperdrive was top priority. Captain Solo told Threepio to interface with the ship's computer brain and find the cause of the malfunctioning motivator. A sudden lurch sent everyone reeling. **"Sir,"** Threepio offered, **"it's quite possible this asteroid is not entirely stable."** Solo snorted with derision. "Not entirely stable? Well, I'm glad you're here to tell us these things." On his captain's orders, Chewbacca roughly grabbed the protocol droid and dragged him aft in the direction of the tech station. **"Oh!"** protested Threepio. **"Sometimes I just don't understand human behavior! After all, I'm only trying to do my job."**

Threepio wasn't looking forward to communicating with the onboard systems of such a disreputable spacecraft. The *Millennium Falcon* possessed no fewer than three distinct droid brains, and

010010101

1001110100

each one seemed to outdo the others in expressing impertinence and discourtesy. Nevertheless, they appeared to operate with an efficiency outside all standardized parameters. Threepio sought out the captain. **"I don't know where your ship learned to communicate,"** he began, **"but it has a most peculiar dialect. I believe, sir, it says that the power coupling on the negative axis has been polarized. I'm afraid you'll have to replace it."** Captain Solo responded with scorn, prompting Threepio to wonder if he'd misdiagnosed the problem. He plugged back into the tech station. It took some time, but his extra effort paid off. Threepio hurried over to the port access corridor, where Captain Solo and the Princess were standing together. **"Sir!"** he said, tapping on the captain's shoulder. **"Sir! I've isolated the reverse power-flux coupling!"** Han turned to regard the interloper. "Thank you," he said. "Thank you very much." **"Oh, you're perfectly welcome, sir,"** replied Threepio, practically glowing with pleasure. Captain Solo was at last beginning to appreciate his talents!

The repairs proceeded apace, but ran into a snag when the Princess discovered a strange creature crawling about on the outer hull. Captain Solo, Leia, and Chewbacca donned breath masks and headed down the *Falcon*'s ramp into the cavern's misty murk. **"I think it might be better if I stay here and guard the ship,"** Threepio announced to the now-empty cabin.

Through the cockpit's transparisteel panes Threepio saw the captain blast one of the ugly brutes, but the commotion roused an entire nest of vermin. A flock of batlike creatures flew past, squealing and flapping leathery wings. **"Oh, go away!"** Threepio shrieked. **"Beastly things! Shoo!"** A sudden tremor knocked him to the deck. As he struggled to his feet, Han Solo shoved him aside and leapt into the pilot's seat. The *Falcon*'s engines whined to life. "Hang on, sweetheart," Han shouted to

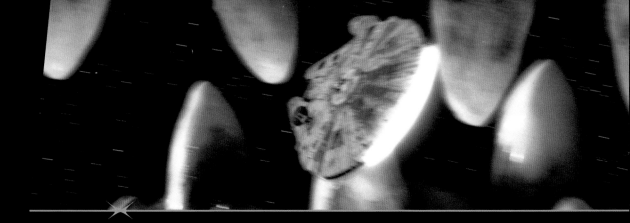

Leia, "we're taking off!" As the ship's repulsors propelled them forward, Threepio spotted two symmetrical rows of what at first appeared to be stalagmites and stalactites framing the cave entrance. The *Millennium Falcon* squeezed through the clamping teeth with meters to spare and rocketed away from the maw of a hungry and angry space slug. As the freighter cleared the asteroid, a pair of TIE scout ships broke orbit and angled back to alert the main Imperial battle fleet.

The *Falcon* sped through the edges of the asteroid field and was once again in open space. A jump into hyperspace was now feasible, if only the Imperials would give them a centimeter of room. Behind them, an Imperial Star Destroyer stayed glued to their stern. Green turbolaser fire raked the cockpit as Captain Solo placed one hand on the hyperdrive levers. "Ready for lightspeed? One, two, three!" The hyperdrive motivator let out a pathetic whine. Threepio risked a glance at the status board just as a laser barrage rocked the ship violently. **"Sir, we just lost the main rear deflector shield! One more hit on the back quarter and we're done for!"** Captain Solo appeared lost in thought, then abruptly ordered Chewbacca to move the ship onto a collision course with their pursuer. See-Threepio could no longer bear it. **"Sir, the odds of surviving a direct assault on an Imperial Star Destroyer—"** Princess Leia, this time, was the one who told him to shut up.

The *Falcon* came about and roared at the Star Destroyer, skimming its gray bulk and rushing past the battleship's bridge. Solo applied the freighter's braking thrusters and looped suicidally around the conning tower. Like a parasitic insect, the *Falcon* attached itself to the aft section of the tower with a magnetized landing claw. **"Captain Solo,"** Threepio burst out, close to hysteria. **"This time you have gone too far!"** Chewbacca let loose a warning growl. **"No, I will *not* be quiet, Chewbacca! Why doesn't anyone *listen* to me?"** As always, the group seemed to take pleasure in ignoring him.

1010010101010101011010100100100101010010010010001001001110100101010100110,

010100101010101010101011010100010\
10101010100101000100100100100100100100100010001001010101001001010101 00.

010010100100100100100100100100101001001001011110101001001001010100101001

THE SAGA OF SEE-THREEPIO

"**Surrender is a perfectly acceptable alternative in extreme circumstances,**" he went on. Princess Leia turned towards him and Threepio felt a momentary surge of hope; surely the Princess saw the wisdom of his words! She placed one hand on the droid's neck. "**The Empire may be gracious enough—**" *Snap*. The tripped circuit breaker cut power to every active and passive system and See-Threepio slipped into oblivion.

He was reactivated by the time the *Millennium Falcon* reached the vaporous planet Bespin. The freighter slipped low through the pink-toned clouds surrounding Cloud City. From the air the floating mining center seemed a paradise of flowing architecture and stunning vistas. Threepio was heartened by the sight. Civilization would be a welcome change from the frontier conditions of Tatooine, Yavin, and Hoth. Cloud City's administrator, a good-natured human by the name of Lando Calrissian, met them at the landing platform. Threepio greeted him warmly. "**Hello, sir. I am See-Threepio, human-cyborg relations. My facilities are at your—**" His voice trailed off as Administrator Calrissian turned on his heel and strode off. Not an auspicious beginning, but then again, he'd received far worse treatment from humans before.

Everything at Cloud City was clean and brightly lit, graceful sculptures hung in wall niches, and industrious citizens bustled past. Threepio lagged behind as he took in the sights. An ornamented door on his right whispered open, revealing a silver-plated protocol unit of the same model as he. "**Oh!**" said Threepio brightly. "**Nice to see a familiar face.**" The droid barely glanced at him. "E chu ta!" it answered, delivering a particularly offensive insult in Huttese. Threepio was completely taken aback, but a moment later he heard the familiar whistling sounds of astromech droidspeak coming from an adjacent corridor. Realizing how much he missed Artoo-Detoo, Threepio stepped down the narrow hallway to have a look.

"Hello? Hello?" he called as he entered a small chamber. He didn't see the R2 unit, but blundered upon a sight he had hoped never to see again: Imperial stormtroopers. "Who are you?" one of them growled. Threepio started to back away, slowly. **"Oh, I'm terribly sorry. I . . . I don't mean to intrude."** The man picked up his rifle from the floor and slowly rose to his feet. **"No, no, please don't get up!"** Threepio shrieked. **"No!"** The trooper leveled his weapon and fired. The last thing Threepio felt was the analog equivalent of nerve-shattering agony.

Internal synapses clicked and popped as they came back online. Threepio's consciousness slipped up, then tumbled back down again as someone adjusted his cognitive matrix. Distantly, he could hear words from his short-term data cache repeating themselves. *Terribly sorry . . . don't mean to intrude . . . no, please don't get up.* His central processor sent a surge of power through the AA-1 VerboBrain, replaying the last few seconds of stored memory. **"Stormtroopers?"** he said, involuntarily. **"Here? We're in danger. I must tell the others. Oh, no! I've been shot!"**

That sudden, horrible memory was tempered by the realization that he had survived the ordeal with his memories intact. Threepio keyed up his photoreceptors and slowly took in his surroundings. He was in a harsh, dark chamber, possibly a security cell. A nearby box held the rest of his body parts. And holding his scorched metal torso upright in two furry paws . . . Chewbacca! Relief was instantaneous and overwhelming. Chewbacca continued his repairs while Threepio offered running advice. **"Oh, yes, that's very good. Well, something's not right, because now I can't see."** When his photoreceptors snapped back on, Threepio attempted to lean forward and check the spot where the stormtrooper's blaster bolt had hit him. **"Wait, wait!"** the protocol droid protested in dismay. **"I'm . . . *backwards!* You stupid furball! Only an overgrown mophead like you would be stupid**

enough—" For the second time in the last few weeks, Threepio's main cutoff switch was tripped. This time, he didn't even see it coming.

When he was reactivated, his half-assembled body was stuffed into a net sack along with his remaining loose limbs, and the whole rattling assembly was strapped to Chewbacca's hairy back. "**If only you'd attached my legs I wouldn't be in this ridiculous position,**" Threepio said peevishly, as the sack bounced up and down with the Wookiee's long loping strides. They were on their way to Cloud City's industrial carbon-freezing facility, where Captain Solo was to be encased in a hibernation shell for delivery to the Tatooine mobster Jabba the Hutt. Though he and Captain Solo hadn't always been on the best of terms, Threepio was deeply saddened by this tragic turn of events.

The full size of the freezing chamber couldn't be discerned through the hanging clouds of steam, but stormtroopers and Ugnaught workers seemed to be everywhere. Observing the scene from atop a high platform stood Darth Vader and the bounty hunter Boba Fett. As Captain Solo descended into the freezing pit Chewbacca turned away in grief, giving his droid passenger a full view of the proceedings. "**Ah, they've encased him in carbonite,**" Threepio observed. Carbonite was a premium alloy highly resistant to shock and extreme temperatures. "**He should be quite well protected. If he survived the freezing process, that is.**" The molten carbonite was flash-frozen and the solid metal slab removed. Lando Calrissian confirmed the vital-sign readouts: the captain was alive and being maintained in a permanent state of stasis.

Boba Fett accompanied Solo's high-tech coffin out of the chamber. The other prisoners were led by stormtrooper escorts towards Vader's Super Star Destroyer. Administrator Calrissian accompanied the grim procession. At the junction of two crossways, a half-dozen blue-uniformed

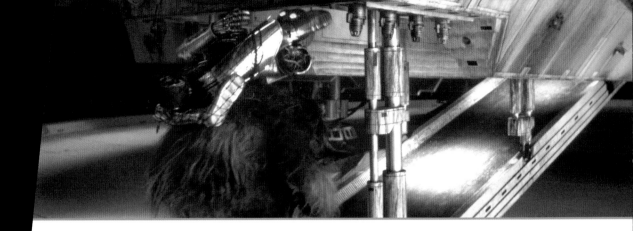

municipal security officers abruptly pulled their weapons and caught the Imperials flat-footed. Calrissian slid in among the stormtroopers, snatching their rifles and issuing terse commands to his cyborg aide. **"I knew all along it had to be a mistake!"** said a relieved See-Threepio. As soon as the binders were released from Chewbacca's wrists, the Wookiee placed both paws around Calrissian's throat and squeezed. Horrified, Threepio called out, **"What are you doing? Trust him! Trust him!"** Chewbacca ignored Threepio, but the Princess succeeded in calming the Wookiee's rage and the two Rebels raced towards Boba Fett's ship. **"I'm terribly sorry about all this,"** Threepio called out to Calrissian. **"After all, he's only a Wookiee!"**

Calrissian caught up with them and led them to the East Platform. On the way, they met a lone, lost astromech droid. Threepio instantly recognized Artoo-Detoo. The little astromech chirruped with happiness as Threepio shouted out his greetings. **"We're trying to save Captain Solo from the bounty hunter!"** he explained. Artoo twittered out a condensed tale of woe. **"At least you're still in one piece,"** Threepio replied. **"Look what happened to me!"**

They reached the East Platform too late. Chewbacca fired several blaster bolts off the hull of Fett's departing *Slave I,* which only alerted the local stormtrooper contingent to the fugitives in their midst. Platform 327 with the waiting *Millennium Falcon* was their only option. Artoo lent valuable assistance to their harrowing escape by laying down a smokescreen as they hustled aboard the freighter. In his haste, Chewbacca bumped Threepio's head repeatedly against the entrance. **"Bend down, you thoughtless . . . ow!"**

The Wookiee dumped him unceremoniously at the top of the ramp, but Artoo-Detoo dragged the net bag into the forward hold. **"I thought that hairy brute would be the end of me,"** wailed

1000100001001001001001010010000100100101010101010
1001010010100101001010010000001010010100101001010011110001001000100111

0011001001010101010

Threepio. Artoo beeped out a banal aside. **"Of course I've looked better!"** Threepio shot back. As the *Falcon* roared away from Cloud City Artoo set to work reattaching his friend's right arm and right leg. The ship rocked with near-hits from laser blasts, and Threepio wondered aloud why they didn't just execute a quick leap into hyperspace. Artoo's knowing answer took him by surprise. **"The city's central computer told you?"** Threepio repeated. **"Artoo-Detoo, you know better than to trust a strange computer."**

Artoo swiveled his head dome and saw Chewbacca frantically tearing at the machinery in a maintenance alcove below decks. Abruptly, he retracted his welding arm and wheeled over to the tech station. **"Artoo, come back at once!"** ordered Threepio. **"I'm standing here in pieces, and you're having delusions of grandeur!"** The little blue astrodroid extended his grasping pincers and seized the manual override lever. A ninety-degree twist nullified the programming block that the Imperial slicers had placed on the ship's hyperdrive motivator. With a ripple of interstellar ether, the *Millennium Falcon* vanished from the realm of realspace. **"You did it!"** shrieked Threepio.

The *Falcon*'s extra-dimensional transit seemed exceptionally long; the Rebel rendezvous point was located far outside the rim of the inhabited galaxy. Upon arrival Master Luke was rushed aboard the medical ship *Redemption* for emergency limb replacement. By the time the surgery was completed, Lando Calrissian and Chewbacca were already preparing to set off on the trail of Boba Fett and his immobilized Corellian captive.

Threepio was sorry to see them go, and Artoo let out a sad whistle. "Take care, you two," Luke said into the comlink. "And may the Force be with you." Through the room's observation window the survivors of Bespin watched their friends depart for places unknown. The *Millennium Falcon*

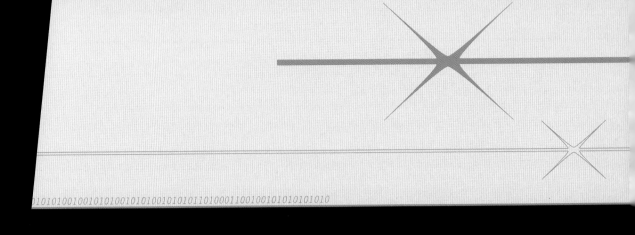

dwindled to an infinitesimal dot and then was swallowed up by the galaxy's swirling stars.

Mere hours after the *Falcon*'s departure, the Rebel fleet was surprised by the appearance of an Imperial strike cruiser. Rogue Squadron's X-wings eliminated the threat with a flurry of proton torpedoes, but their secrecy had been compromised. The armada broke formation and headed back towards the galactic plane.

For the next two months the Rebel Alliance remained on the move. See-Threepio and Artoo-Detoo did their best to help out during these somber times, even saving the Rebel fleet from burning up in Arbra's sun and volunteering for a risky mission to the hostile "droid world" of Kligson's Moon.

Princess Leia's dedication to the Rebel Alliance could not stop her from worrying about Han Solo. When Lando Calrissian and Chewbacca reported that they had uncovered solid information on the Corellian's whereabouts, Leia was granted a temporary leave of absence by Mon Mothma and Admiral Ackbar. The droids accompanied the Princess to Tatooine where Boba Fett was scheduled to arrive with his carbonized prize. The bounty hunter failed to show.

See-Threepio accompanied Princess Leia to an information-gathering mission on Rodia. Later, he remained behind with Lando Calrissian aboard the *Millennium Falcon* as the other Rebel heroes split up to perform various missions. Threepio enjoyed his brief time with Captain Calrissian, finding the former administrator to be a true gentleman with refined tastes and educated opinions.

Eventually Captain Calrissian and Threepio picked up Master Luke and Artoo-Detoo and made a hyperspace hop to Coruscant. Here, in the capital of the Empire, the two humans hoped to rescue Princess Leia from the most heavily guarded personal residence in the galaxy, following Leia's dis-

astrous attempt to infiltrate Prince Xizor's castle. Threepio was ordered to remain behind with the ship, and for once he could detect no flaws in human logic. When a threatening gang of armed men approached the ship—some manner of local thugs or enforcers—Master Luke, via comlink, ordered the droids to power up and get out while they could. Artoo-Detoo could handle the engines and navigation, but Threepio's humanoid configuration required that he man the control yoke. The *Falcon* smashed into holo-billboards and narrowly averted collision with a sky-hook tether on its way across Imperial City. The droids finally arrived at Prince Xizor's castle, where they rendezvoused with the others. Threepio was surprised to feel a twinge of reluctance when he surrendered the controls to Captain Calrissian.

The Alliance's spies soon learned that Boba Fett had delivered Han Solo's body to Jabba the Hutt. Since Jabba's palace was regarded as impregnable, successful extrication would be extremely difficult. Princess Leia and See-Threepio returned to Tatooine in a two-seat Y-wing and rendezvoused with the other Rebel rescuers at Ben Kenobi's hut for long days of planning. Eventually they moved the Y-wing, Master Luke's X-wing, and the *Millennium Falcon* to a spot in the Dune Sea just outside Jabba's sensor range. Captain Calrissian and Chewbacca departed to scout out the cast-iron fortress, and several days later the droids were told to journey there on foot to deliver an important message to Jabba himself.

The last time he had trudged across the sands of Tatooine, Threepio had almost expired from circuit meltdown. This time the path was easier and the morning temperature considerably cooler. Before long the palace of Jabba the Hutt came into view. See-Threepio couldn't imagine the purpose of traveling all this way to play a simple holo-recording. **"Lando Calrissian and poor Chewbacca**

00100101001010010100101001000000101

never returned from this awful place," he commented to Artoo. "**If I told you half the things I've heard about this Jabba the Hutt, you'd probably short-circuit.**"

The two droids were ushered into the receiving chamber, where Threepio found that his fears had been greatly understated. The lowest dregs of galactic civilization skulked in the shadowy alcoves, and overlooking it all from a raised dais—like a severed tongue on a serving platter—sat Jabba the Hutt. Artoo played Master Luke's holographic recording without preamble. The three-meter hologram requested an appointment with Jabba to discuss the ownership of Captain Solo's slab. Then the hologram dropped a bombshell. "As a token of my goodwill, I present to you a gift: these two droids. Both are hardworking, and will serve you well."

Threepio was in shock. As he was led through the dungeons by a pair of piggish Gamorreans, the extent of his predicament began to sink in. Threepio emerged in a robotic chamber of horrors overseen by a sadistic taskmaster. "**Artoo, don't leave me!**" Threepio cried out, but he was forcibly dragged away. Before long, he had become the official interpreter for the galaxy's most vile criminal.

Jabba the Hutt's seething cesspool of a throne room was the nadir of Threepio's entire protocol career. Thugs, gunrunners, murderers, and spice addicts—every last one was an uncivilized barbarian. In their eyes Threepio saw hard pitiless contempt and imagined they would like nothing more than to pound the new protocol droid into golden ingots. Or, at least, to stand by and wait for the amusing moment when Jabba decided to disintegrate his newest appropriation.

Not every denizen of the palace was in a position of power. There were other slaves and servants like himself, whose lives rested on the whims and appetites of their powerful master. Threepio

struck up conversations with two of the dancing girls, Oola and Arica, but Oola was soon dropped into a pit and devoured by Jabba's pet rancor. Moments later, blaster shots and sounds of struggle echoed from the corridor. The source of the commotion proved to be a helmeted bounty hunter—Ubese, by his dress and speech—leading a Wookiee prisoner by a chain. **"Oh, no! Chewbacca!"** Threepio said, horrified. This, then, was the end to Master Luke's plan. Bounty hunters had tracked down the Rebel heroes. He only hoped Master Luke and the Princess had escaped.

The new arrival conducted his bounty negotiations with audacity. Ubese were a species known for their boldness, but brandishing a ticking thermal detonator while trapped in a locked room was a bit over the top. Eventually the manhunter was offered an acceptable price and Chewbacca was dragged off to the dungeons. Throughout the translation session Jabba only knocked Threepio from the dais once, a marginally better outcome than the droid had feared.

Perhaps, Threepio hoped, Jabba would delay disintegrating him until tomorrow.

The rest of the day Threepio kept to himself. He worried about the fate of Artoo and clung to the increasingly unlikely prospect of a last-minute rescue by Master Luke. As the evening's tipsy carousal wound down to a whimper, Threepio was appalled to see that most of the revelers simply slouched in a corner and dropped off to sleep. He wouldn't have dared to touch that floor without a beam-cleaner and a drum of industrial disinfectant. A few hours later, Threepio was approached by Bib Fortuna. He wanted to ask the majordomo when he would be allowed an oil bath or at least a good recharge session, but the Twi'lek activated his restraining bolt before he could speak a single word. Fortuna led him behind a curtain into an alcove near Captain Solo's slab, where several of the more alert courtiers were already assembling.

Jabba, recently awakened from his own slumber, sat in the center of the gathering like a swollen Tervissian tick. Fortuna peeked furtively through the edges of the tapestry and gave the signal to throw the curtain wide. There, at the center of the chamber floor in Ubese gear was Princess Leia, and next to her, a reanimated Han Solo. The Hutt's toadies and snivelers exploded with mirth, their hollow cackles resounding off the chamber walls. A pair of Gamorreans forcibly towed Captain Solo to his dungeon cell. The Princess was thrown forward to land on Jabba's greasy rolls as the Hutt extended his tongue with lecherous desire. See-Threepio averted his face in disgust. **"Oh, I can't bear to watch,"** he moaned, but the words were swallowed up in a fresh cacophony of celebration.

The night seemed endless, but fresh optimism arrived at daybreak. Master Luke, dressed in a wizard's black robes, stepped confidently into the chamber of his dangerous enemy. Threepio couldn't contain his glee. **"At last, Master Luke's come to rescue me!"** Luke's cool blue eyes took in the room in an instant, briefly locking gazes with Leia in her humiliating position as human accessory. Threepio watched the negotiations anxiously, and when things started to go poorly he called out a warning. **"Master Luke, you're standing on—"** Jabba's thundering voice drowned out his words, and before he could do anything Luke had fallen headlong into the rancor's lair. Like every rancor feeding Threepio had been forced to witness, the struggle was over quickly. But this time the outcome was completely different. The freakish monster gave a tiny cry of pain as it breathed its last.

Jabba's roar of rage was deafening. Luke and Han were presented to the mighty gangster for the pronouncement of their death orders. Threepio translated the dire news as accurately as possible, dreadful as it was. **"The great Jabba the Hutt has decreed that you are to be terminated**

immediately," he began. **"You will therefore be taken to the Dune Sea and cast into the Pit of Carkoon, the nesting place of the all-powerful Sarlacc."** Threepio listened to Jabba's next sentence and ran through it twice to make sure he wasn't imagining things. Dutifully, he plowed on. **"In his belly you will find a new definition of pain and suffering, as you are slowly digested over a . . . thousand years."** The prisoners were led away, and Luke shouted to Jabba that this whole affair was the last mistake the Hutt would ever make. Threepio didn't know whether to be reassured by Master Luke's blind faith or terrified by the fact that the poor human had lost his mind.

The Hutt was nothing if not extravagant. Most of the Imperial officers Threepio had encountered over the years would have eliminated a captured prisoner on the spot; Jabba arranged a raucous all-day execution party and sightseeing trip. The call went out to the palace's staff: fuel the sail barge, stock the wet bar, load the musicians' instruments, prepare enough food for three dozen individuals—and then cook a few extra dishes so Jabba's guests would have something to eat as well.

The sail barge would have been roomy under normal conditions, but that day it was packed so thickly with drunken ruffians that Threepio could scarcely move without treading on someone's tentacle. To make matters worse, the vessel's rhythmic rocking was making him acutely queasy. He made a note to have his gyroscopic balance modules realigned at the earliest possible opportunity. As he sidestepped an alien with a whiskered face and overpowering breath, he crashed into a small drink-service robot and nearly knocked it on its side. **"Artoo!"** he cried out in surprise and relief. In spite of all that had gone wrong with the plan to rescue Captain Solo, it was heartening to see that at least one friend would still be with him at the conclusion of this bleak day. Artoo whistled out a bit of optimistic cheer. **"I wish I had your confidence,"** Threepio replied doubtfully.

Jabba's booming voice cut through the ambient chatter. Flinching at the word "talkdroid," See-Threepio scrambled to his master's side, shouting out apologies for his absence. Through the sail barge's louvered windows he saw the Great Pit of Carkoon, where, one by one, Master Luke, Captain Solo, and Chewbacca would be forced to walk the plank. Jabba chortled with despicable glee. **"Victims of the almighty Sarlacc,"** Threepio translated, his words amplified by a loudspeaker horn. **"His Excellency hopes that you will die honorably. But should any of you wish to beg for mercy, the great Jabba the Hutt will now listen to your pleas."** Captain Solo did indeed have a few words to share, but Threepio didn't see how he could possibly relay them without being thrown into the pit himself. Jabba took a few moments to savor the situation, licked his gluey lips, then ordered his men to begin the executions.

Threepio averted his face as Master Luke stepped off the gangplank, and assumed the deafening roar that erupted from the sail barge was a depraved cheer of triumph. But when he finally dared to look, Master Luke was cutting a path of devastation through Jabba's gang with a glowing green lightsaber. The Hutt roared with rage as his henchmen rushed to battle stations. Princess Leia, characteristically clear-headed, ordered the golden droid to hand her a heavy ornamental sculpture, then brought the statue down on the Hutt's instrument panel, cutting power to the window panels and plunging the barge into darkness. As Jabba's guards raced about in confusion, she looped her chain around the Hutt's neck and pulled.

Threepio found Artoo-Detoo and led him back towards Jabba's dais, knowing the astromech's arc welder could snap the metal links that held the Princess captive. As Artoo rolled forward, the contemptible little monkey-lizard Salacious Crumb hopped up on a console and tossed a

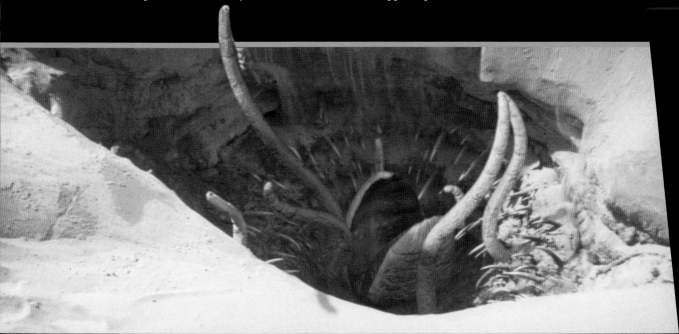

dessert plate at Leia's head. Shouting and waving his arms in a threatening manner, Threepio rushed headlong at the horrible beast. Crumb sprang forward and landed on Threepio's face with such force he clattered backwards onto the deck. Salacious Crumb's ugly visage loomed large as the pest leaned forward to take a bite out of Threepio's right photoreceptor. By the time Artoo came to the rescue, the monster had torn loose the entire optical assembly with his sharp beak. **"Oh, my eye! Artoo, help!"** A zap from Artoo's arc welder sent the animal scooting up into the rafters. Both droids followed Princess Leia's lead and hurried above deck into the light of Tatooine's twin suns.

Master Luke was taking out Jabba's thugs one by one. See-Threepio caught only a glimpse of the furious lightsaber combat before Artoo stupidly herded him to the edge of the upper deck. A fall from this height would be suicide! **"Artoo, where are we going?"** he began. **"I couldn't possibly ju—"** Just as he was working up a logical protest, the devious little trickster plowed into his legs and sent him pitching helplessly over the side. Threepio managed to squeak out one terrified yelp and then he hit the hot sand headfirst, plowing into the slack dune all the way up to his knees. He was just beginning to work up a good froth of self-pity when something affixed itself to his legs with a metallic clack. A cargo hoist jerked him free, but now he was dangling upside down dozens of meters above the ground. The exploding sail barge ejected razor-sharp hull fragments and spat geysers of flame in every direction. *Will this never end?* he wondered, for at least the twenty-second time since morning recharge.

There wasn't even time for a proper goodbye to Artoo-Detoo. After arriving back at the vehicle encampment in the middle of a sandstorm, Artoo and Master Luke departed in their X-wing and

C-3PO: TALES OF THE GOLDEN DROID

the *Millennium Falcon* headed back to the Rebel fleet; wind damage had rendered the Y-wing fighter inoperable. Captain Solo "repaired" Threepio's damaged photoreceptor by stuffing it back into his optical socket. Without the proper recalibration for depth perception, the droid found himself bumping into bulkheads.

It wasn't a droid's place to criticize, but Threepio felt hurt that he had been excluded from the rescue plan. Everyone else in the group—*especially* Artoo-Detoo—had been entrusted with an essential covert role. Over the years hadn't Threepio proven his worth to the Rebel Alliance more times than he could count? The Princess explained that it was *precisely* his unrehearsed artlessness that had convinced Jabba to allow the droids into his entourage. Without Threepio to allay Jabba's suspicions, the entire plan would have crumbled like a delicately balanced sabacc deck. Leia's sound explanation made Threepio feel considerably better. What's more, Captain Calrissian helped him retune his faulty photoreceptor.

The armada in the Sullust system was by far the largest gathering of warships the Rebel Alliance had ever assembled. Aboard the headquarters vessel *Home One*, Threepio attended a strategy briefing for the top Rebel officers and learned of the Empire's latest military bauble, a second, more powerful Death Star. General Calrissian and General Solo would head up the sabotage mission; Han would eliminate the battle station's shield generator on the forest moon of Endor, enabling Lando's starfighters to destroy the Death Star. When Solo called for volunteers to join his crew, Master Luke appeared through the open hatchway. "I'm with you, too," he called, to the cheers of the other Rebels. Threepio pushed his way through the crowd to greet Artoo-Detoo, who beeped out a ten-second recap of his recent voyage and twittered enthusiastically about the exciting adventure still to come. Threepio

sniffed with indifference. **"Exciting is hardly the word I would use."**

No force in the galaxy could keep Artoo-Detoo from the Endor mission, but Threepio surprised himself by volunteering. He was reluctant to be left behind, but he also discovered that his sense of duty had deepened during his trials on Tatooine. Threepio boarded the stolen Imperial shuttle *Tydirium* with the rest of the command crew as Major Derlin and his elite commando unit filed into the crew compartment. The graceful tri-winged transport hopped from Sullust to an uninhabited layover system, and from there to the forest moon of Endor.

See-Threepio sampled the crisp, chilly air with his olfactory detector as he stepped from the shuttle's ramp onto the great green surface of the moon. Immediately he identified decaying timber, mold spores, rich loamy soil, animal droppings, sweet tree sap, and sixteen distinct varieties of flowering plant. A human would describe the scent as pleasantly woodsy, but it was all too raw for his liking. Threepio followed Major Derlin's commandos through the forest to a rendezvous with General Solo, who silently indicated the presence of Imperial scouts over the next rise. The ensuing spontaneous sneak attack was a disaster. Master Luke and the Princess hijacked a high-speed repulsor bike and rocketed into the forest, pursuing two fleeing Imperials, and the remaining group settled down to await their return.

Luke and Leia showed no signs of coming back, and General Solo's comlink was unable to punch through an area-wide jamming field. After an intolerable stretch of waiting, Luke returned, alone and on foot. General Solo ordered Derlin's commandos ahead to the shield generator, and the rest of the crew headed off into the woods to find the lost Princess. Artoo-Detoo spun his auxiliary sensor dish in sweeping search patterns, and eventually picked up on the ruined remains of a speeder bike.

"**I'm afraid that Artoo's sensors can find no trace of Princess Leia,**" Threepio said. Moments later, Chewbacca discovered a butchered lump of fur and fangs hanging limply from a dead tree. Luke sensed imminent danger and tried to prevent Chewie from shaking the bait, but it was too late. With a *sproing* of released tension, a net trap enveloped the group, hauling them several meters above the ground.

Artoo slid open a chassis compartment and extended his circular cutting saw. "**Artoo, I'm not sure that's such a good idea,**" Threepio said, as the saw severed the net's primary strand and adjacent cords began to stretch and snap. "**It's a very long—*droooop!***" Threepio hit the forest floor with such force it scrambled the gyro-balance circuitry in his cranial unit. And someone, most likely Chewbacca, used him as an impromptu landing cushion. It took a moment to clear the glitches from his cognitive matrix. "**Oh, my head,**" he moaned as he sat up, only to find himself surrounded by a sea of brown, furry primitives.

"**Oh, my goodness,**" he exclaimed, as the creatures prostrated themselves in the dirt and performed reverential bows in his direction. Threepio ran the creatures' speech through his language database. There were no direct matches, but several extinct dialects appeared close enough in syntax for him to formulate a reply. After a brief exchange, he explained the situation to his companions. These creatures, the Ewoks, believed he was their golden sun god, come to walk among his worshippers in corporeal form. Captain Solo's jaw fell open in disbelief. "Well, why don't you use your divine influence and get us out of this?" he suggested. Threepio drew himself up, offended. "**Begging your pardon, General Solo, but that just wouldn't be proper. It's against my programming to imperson-ate a deity.**"

110010100100100101010

1010001000010010010010000101001000010010010101010101010100101001010011110001001000100111111111110010010010010
0101010010100101010010100101001000010100100101001010010100101001001001010010010010010111

10100101110101010010001001010000000010010100100101000010100101001010010010010010100101001010010101001010010101000100100101001010101010

The Ewoks constructed a throne of timber and twine for their golden god and bore it on their shoulders. The other Rebels were lashed to poles and toted up to the platforms and cat-walks of a precarious treetop village. The procession halted at the entrance to the largest hut, where Threepio's pallet was placed in a position of honor. A bevy of high-ranking Ewoks came out to congratulate the hunting party. The two senior figures appeared to be Logray, the village medicine man, and Chief Chirpa, the tribe's warlord. Logray stepped forward to address the Ewoks' god incarnate.

"I'm rather embarrassed, General Solo," Threepio called out to the others, whose stakes were being positioned above fire pits, **"but it appears you are to be the main course at a banquet in my honor."** Threepio gathered that the Ewoks viewed his friends as Imperial soldiers. In fact, the Ewoks assumed their glittering god had descended from the sky strictly so he could deliver these enemies into the hands of his followers. In keeping with an ancient tradition Logray planned to roast the prisoners to make a meal for the Ewok warriors, a ceremony to venerate the visiting god and give the warriors the fighting strength of their fallen foes. The Ewoks might be ferocious head-hunters but, frankly, Threepio was finding their constant attention rather flattering.

Princess Leia, dressed in a garment woven from local fabric, appeared in the doorway of the main hut. The Rebel heroes shouted with relief. Leia gestured angrily towards the cooking pits. "Threepio, tell them they must be set free." The protocol droid obeyed, but received an uncooperative reply. Because an Ewok scout named Wicket had helped the Princess fight off stormtroopers, she was considered a friend of the tribe. The other Rebels had not proven themselves in like fashion.

See-Threepio was becoming anxious, but Master Luke remained glacially calm. Luke

0010000100100100100010100100000100100101010101010100010100101001111000100100010011111111111001001010010010100000101001001010
0100101001010100101001010100101001

001010010010010101010010010010001001

instructed Threepio to warn the Ewoks of the consequences of defying a god, an ultimatum which the protocol droid delivered with reluctance. It really *was* against his programming to impersonate a deity, and of course there was no way to follow through on an empty threat like "magic." Suddenly, Threepio's chair shuddered with intangible power and rose into the air. Threepio cried out for help as his throne mysteriously revolved in a full circle. At last the wooden chair settled gently to the ground and a worshipful Chief Chirpa ordered the prisoners' immediate release. **"I never knew I had it in me,"** muttered Threepio.

A few hours later the stars had come out in Endor's night sky. The Ewoks were eager to learn more about their offworld guests and to put the misunderstanding behind them, so Luke appointed See-Threepio as the Rebels' official teller of tales. Threepio was flattered by Master Luke's confidence, since he knew he had no natural talent for storytelling.

Nearly a hundred Ewoks packed Chief Chirpa's hut to listen to the tale. See-Threepio stood in the center next to the heating fire, pantomiming the actions of Master Luke, General Solo, and the other heroes who had made his life so disordered over the past four years. His six-million-language vocabulator could reproduce nearly any sound, and he peppered the monologue with roaring X-wings and plodding AT-ATs. To his delight, the Ewoks hung on his every word. When he finished, Chief Chirpa consulted briefly with the Council of Elders and delivered a proclamation to the assembled gathering. **"Wonderful!"** Threepio exclaimed. **"We are now part of the tribe."**

The next morning an Ewok scouting party, led by Paploo and Wicket, took the Rebels to the Imperial bunker that powered the Death Star's shield generator. Here they reconnected with Major Derlin and his team of strike commandos. The bunker's entrance was too heavily guarded for a straight-

on assault, but an Ewok tip led the Rebels through the forest to a secret rear entrance guarded by only four troopers. Paploo drew off three of them by hijacking a speeder bike, and the remaining scout was an easy mark. Minutes later, Han Solo entered the scout trooper's surrendered passcode and the bunker doors rumbled open. From their hiding spot atop a forested knoll, Threepio and Artoo watched the Rebel saboteurs vanish into the enemy installation.

Artoo-Detoo whistled that it should take less than ten minutes for the squad to place their charges, set the timers, and evacuate. Threepio fidgeted anxiously. Suddenly the leaves in front of him seemed to melt into the form of an Ewok warrior. Startled, Threepio cried out, but it was only Paploo, freshly returned from his speeder bike adventure. Paploo chattered rapidly to Wicket, and Threepio could only make out a handful of terms: white shell, lightning spear, *toron togosh*.

In the next instant a pair of Imperial speeder bikes shot out of the brush at the far side of the bunker clearing. The scouts quickly reconnoitered the area, then vanished back the way they had come. A few heartbeats later they reappeared at the head of a column of stormtroopers. **"Oh, my!"** Threepio burst out, horrified, as a squad of the troopers filed through the bunker doors with precise military discipline. He turned towards Wicket for moral support, but the little Ewok was fleeing headlong into the brush. More speeder bikes joined the stormtrooper battalion and two-legged Imperial scout walkers stomped towards the clearing, flattening green saplings with every tread.

By now all the Ewoks had vanished into the forest. Threepio could hardly blame them for being faint-hearted in the face of such overwhelming odds. He looked around for Artoo-Detoo and panicked when the little droid was nowhere to be found. Moments later his friend emerged from a shadowed thicket, beeping excitedly. With trepidation, See-Threepio agreed to his counterpart's

1000101001000010010010101010101010100101001010100101001

mysterious request. Sometimes trust was the only constant currency in a hopeless situation.

"**Hello!**" Threepio called. Leia and the other Rebel prisoners, under guard in the center of the clearing, looked around in confusion. "**I say, over there!**" Threepio continued, as dozens of white-helmeted heads fixed on his position. "**Were you looking for me?**" An Imperial officer shouted an order and a line of stormtroopers trotted up the ridge towards the golden droid, weapons held at the ready. "**Artoo,**" Threepio said softly, paralyzed by sudden self-doubt, "**are you sure this was a good idea?**" But then the troopers were upon them and there was no time for second thoughts.

A band of Ewoks sprung from the trees like furry demons and overwhelmed the Imperial soldiers, beating them savagely with wooden clubs. Simultaneously a distant blast from a war horn signaled the primary attack, and the Rebels' stormtrooper guards—caught in a perfect crossfire with no cover for a dozen meters—were decimated by a blizzard of spears and arrows. Artoo-Detoo extended his auxiliary tread and rolled resolutely towards the center of the storm. "**Going?**" Threepio repeated. "**What do you mean, you're going? This is no time for heroics! Come back!**" The panicky protocol droid performed a quick calculation and determined that crossing the clearing was eminently preferable to being left alone on the ridge. Threepio gathered his nerve and raced through a web of crisscrossing blaster fire to the safety of the bunker door.

General Solo and Princess Leia were already there. Artoo scooted up to the door's control panel and plugged in, cycling through the Imperial computer's stored passcodes. An Imperial sharpshooter caught the little droid with a laser bolt, blasting him away from the computer socket with such force that he bounced off the opposite wall. Solo's answering shot dropped the sniper. "**My goodness!**"

cried Threepio, who hadn't taken his eyes off poor Artoo. The heroic astromech sparked, smoked, and sputtered as a cascading power overload popped open the doors to every chassis compartment. Artoo's self-preservation safeties kicked in and he slipped into automated unconsciousness. **"Why did you have to be so brave?"** his oldest friend lamented.

The rest of the battle was a blur to Threepio, preoccupied as he was with the fate of Artoo-Detoo. Eventually Chewbacca poked his head out from a captured scout walker and roared the happy news: The Ewoks had scattered the stormtrooper army and destroyed every last piece of Imperial heavy equipment. General Solo tricked the Imperial bunker commander into reopening the back doors, and Solo and Major Derlin's commandos placed the sequencer charges. See-Threepio was well out of sight when the installation blew, but the force and fire of the colossal explosion was felt for kilometers.

There was nothing more to be accomplished on Endor's surface. The Rebels moved farther back into the woods and Major Derlin turned custody of their stormtrooper prisoners over to Paploo and the vigilant Ewok warriors. Han and Leia took turns looking though Derlin's electrobinoculars at the flashing dots of the space battle high overhead. See-Threepio commandeered the services of a Rebel technician, who patiently ran a diagnostic on Artoo-Detoo and recharged his systems motivator. The tech's prognosis was positive.

A collective gasp prompted Threepio to glance up at the blue sky. The unblinking eye of the Death Star, which had been looming above them like an omen of doom since the day they arrived, was no more. In its place, a blossom of wavy streamers burst across the heavens in a silent eruption. Hoarse shouts of triumph reverberated throughout the forest. **"They did it!"** exulted Threepio.

Nightfall brought with it a riotous celebration. Rebel shuttles and starfighters touched down in the forest and disgorged pilots who packed the Ewoks' treetop village with high spirits and camaraderie. The Emperor was dead, the Imperial fleet was on the run, and the Rebel Alliance had captured two Star Destroyers. Everyone had reasons to celebrate. Even See-Threepio found himself dancing with an enthusiastic young Ewok. Chief Chirpa, a gracious host, provided music and windenberry wine until the early morning hours.

It seemed as if all the excitement and adventures had finally come to an end, but Threepio knew he could never be so lucky. The next day, a distress beacon arrived from the remote planet Bakura, and the Rebels went immediately to their aid. The frontier world was under siege by a mysterious, intelligent reptilian species from the Unknown Regions. The Bakurans called them Fluties, but their proper name was the Ssi-ruuk, and See-Threepio's greatest achievement during the temporary Empire/Alliance truce was the translation of the aliens' musical language. Threepio's interpretations were used as templates by the Alliance military, allowing them to understand and operate captured Ssi-ruuk equipment including the capital ship, *Sibwarra*.

The Rebel Alliance morphed into the New Republic, and See-Threepio's duties became more political. Princess Leia took on responsibilities within the governmental hierarchy and frequently needed Threepio's services as a translator or personal aide. Artoo-Detoo spent most of his time with Master Luke and his X-wing fighter, but the two droids still saw each other in the corridors of the traveling flagship *Home One*.

After long years of struggle the New Republic succeeded in capturing Coruscant, the seat of galactic power. At last there were civilized surroundings in which to conduct legitimate diplomacy!

Threepio was truly in his element. Then, General Solo spoiled everything in his inimitable fashion by hijacking everyone to the uncharted wilderness of Dathomir. They barely escaped the wretched planet with their lives, and Threepio's shocking discovery that Han Solo was the hereditary king of Corellia proved to be an empty fraud. The impudent smuggler added insult to injury by wedding Princess Leia.

When the Imperial menace reappeared in the person of Grand Admiral Thrawn, See-Threepio accompanied the Princess on a harrowing mission to the Noghri homeworld of Honoghr. Soon after, forces loyal to Emperor Palpatine's clone threw themselves at the New Republic with astonishing vigor. The Imperials quickly recaptured Coruscant, but the New Republic rebounded and the capital planet changed hands once more. Thousands of volunteers set to work repairing the extensive battle damage to Imperial City. Meanwhile, See-Threepio had bigger problems on his hands. Their names were Jacen, Jaina, and Anakin.

Princess Leia Organa Solo's three children were more than a handful. Their budding Force abilities made them impossible to control, but Threepio did his best as the Organa family nanny. When the children grew to school age, See-Threepio returned to his duties in protocol. He occasionally took time out for adventures with his old friend Artoo-Detoo, such as the time Captain Calrissian stranded them all aboard a mysterious ghost ship built by Qella aliens.

To this day See-Threepio stays busy as ever, with an endless string of state dinners, cultural performances, and inauguration ceremonies on behalf of the New Republic government. He even helped Chewbacca design and program Em Teedee, a miniaturized translation droid for Chewie's nephew Lowbacca. Artoo-Detoo is currently assigned to Luke Skywalker's Jedi academy on Yavin 4, but

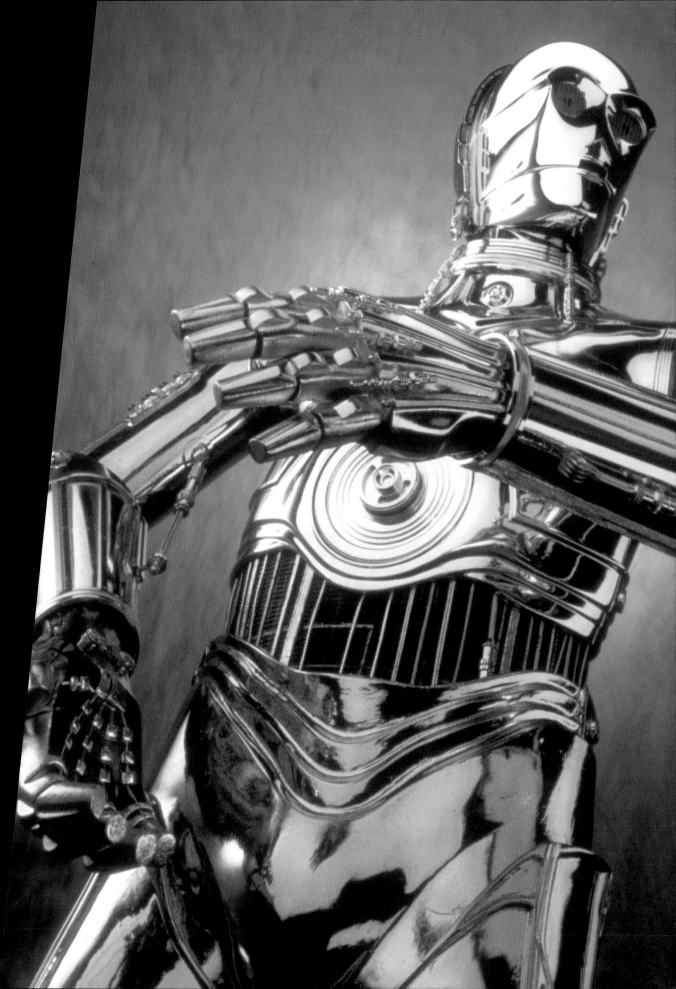

the two friends make an effort to see each other every few weeks. In short, his life is as blissful as a droid's can be. But Threepio has a knack for seeing shadows on the sunniest days, and in this case, he might be right. Ominous storm clouds seem to be gathering on the horizon, portents of a cyclone that could sweep across the New Republic and leave ruins in its wake. If disaster does strike, it will run up against a frail, golden protocol droid never built for combat, standing up bravely for his friends in spite of the raging winds.

If you have a bunch of action figures, you need a place to keep them. This beautifully designed, vacuum-metalized C-3PO carrying case filled the bill for Kenner in 1983.

III: GOLDEN TREASURES:
C-3PO COLLECTIBLES

When C-3PO joyously exclaims to R2-D2, "Thank the maker!" is he talking about Hasbro or perhaps Don Post Studios? When R2-D2 calls the golden droid "a mindless philosopher," has he just finished reading *C-3PO's Book about Robots* from Random House or *Droids: The Kalarba Adventure* from Dark Horse Comics? When the bartender at a certain Mos Eisley cantina takes one look at "Goldenrod" and his squat companion and sneers, "We don't serve their kind here," what wouldn't he serve: a Burger Chef Threepio Funmeal or a droid-head candy sucker from Australia? From kids' underwear to holographic watches, chocolate lollipops to sweetened cereal, and taco bags to pizza boxes—it sometimes seems that the world has gone crazy for probably the most recognizable robot, droid, or mechanical man of the twentieth century.

The inspired creation of Threepio, with the mannerisms of a mime, the voice of a fussy British butler, and the attitude that it's his "lot in life" to suffer has endeared him to millions, thanks in no small part to British actor Anthony Daniels, the man behind the mask. And C-3PO's appearance in Episode I of the vast *Star Wars* saga, even though relatively brief and more as See-Throughpio than See-Threepio, has kept him alive in the hearts and minds of consumers and collectors. There are good reasons for Threepio's megasuccess in the merchandising arena. For one thing, he's one of the good guys, even a bit of a hero despite his sometimes timid and cautious demeanor. It's also a lot easier to sculpt the face of a character already a mask than it is to produce an accurate rendition of a human. And Threepio's voice is so recognizable that it has been used on everything from public service television spots warning about the hazards of smoking to CD-ROMs guiding players through computer games.

C-3PO figurines made of plastic, rubber, and metal are numerous and come in many sizes. This 1998 Threepio beanbag "Buddy" from Hasbro is the first plush version of the protocol droid to be sold in the US.

In 1977 Weingeroff Enterprises produced many pieces of jewelry with Threepio's full figure or bust. Girls could wear the droid on their fingers, around their necks, on their ears (pierced or not), on their wrists, or, with this C-3PO barrette, even in their hair.

Because C-3PO and R2-D2 were designed from the start as a team, partly to help frame the story of *Star Wars* and partly to provide comic relief, much of the licensed merchandise also pairs them. Early on, there was a Bradley Time dimensional clock where Artoo beeps and whistles and C-3PO uses his persuasive power to wake up the "young Rebel." More recently, Thinkway produced a marvelous battery-operated bank with a C-3PO figure that talks and moves and an R2-D2 that lights up and rolls forward to "kick" the coin into a slot. The merchandise highlighted in this chapter's list and photos mostly uses Threepio by himself. The list would be twice as long if it included merchandise using both droids.

A C-3PO collection, or some souvenirs of the golden droid's exploits, needn't be expensive. Items start at just a few coins for a small plastic candy-filled head or an individual trading card. At the other extreme is a full-sized, light-up replica from Don Post Studios, which retails for up to $7,500! It may be expensive, but it's as close to the real thing as most people will ever get. If that's too much of a budget breaker, small scale build-it-yourself model kits have been available since 1978 from more than a half-dozen different companies around the world.

Among the first Threepio items available when *Star Wars* premiered in the United States in late spring 1977 were T-shirts and posters from Factors Inc. and an extensive line of inexpensive jewelry from Weingeroff Ent., including barrettes, bracelets, earrings, pendants, pins, and rings. In England one company had the license to do high-end sterling silver and gold jewelry but sold only a limited number of pieces. It wasn't until J.A.P. Inc. of Japan entered the picture in 1997 with an exquisitely sculpted series of large rings that the droid appeared on high-end jewelry again. J.A.P. offered a silver, a gold-plated, and a 24-karat solid gold version of the Threepio ring. The latter was limited to fifty copies worldwide and cost more than $2,000.

Without a doubt the largest production of any one item has been the C-3PO collector figure, first from Kenner and its worldwide affiliates and now from Hasbro, which purchased Kenner several years ago. The first C-3PO figure came on a so-called *Star Wars* twelveback card in 1978. The problem with Threepio, as opposed to Princess Leia or even Luke Skywalker, is that he always looks the same, so there was only one basic figure. Kenner did manage to come up with one main variation: a C-3PO with removable limbs and a net for Chewbacca to carry them in.

The true collector, however, can always find a few more variations, whether it's the card front or back, a related line, or even a foreign market change. For a small line of action figures based on the *Droids* animated television show in 1985, Kenner produced a Threepio with a cartoonlike paint job and put it on a card with a coin. There were variations on the coin. The first one released was a duplicate of the coin from the regular Power of the Force line. Later it was changed to one picturing the animated Threepio.

In Japan, the head of the original Threepio was resculpted before it was released on a card that included a Takara paper sticker. Nearly twenty years later, the Japanese market got another variation as authorities feared that the regular gold vacuum plating on the figure might make it too brittle for young children. After an initial small batch was released, Hasbro used a different process that gave the figure more of a greenish-gold tint. In the United States, Hasbro managed to come up with a few more variations on the classic Threepio by tweaking either the sculpt or the paint job on the figure for the newer Power of the Force line that appeared in 1995.

Threepio seems to have engendered more ceramic collectibles than any other character. The 1983 C-3PO tape dispenser from Sigma is one of the more unusual pieces, and one that gives Threepio's alter ego, actor Anthony Daniels, a great punch line.

C-3PO is featured on several pieces from Hollywood Pins. This 1995 enameled pinback comes with one of Threepio's most famous lines from the first Star Wars trilogy.

Threepio has graced food packages worldwide since the first film appeared. He's an easy and recognizable character to use. While using a character whose expression never changes can be a challenge, it can also be a plus since consumers from scores of different cultures can read into that golden visage anything they want. See-Threepio has been used to sell sweetened cereal, pizza, Mexican food, hamburgers, Coca-Cola and its arch-rival Pepsi, cookies, chocolates, marshmallows, bread, juice, dozens of varieties of salty snacks, jelly candies, lollipops, cakes, juice drinks, yogurt, and ice cream treats, from England to Australia.

Of all the items, one of the strangest came from Sigma, which produced a beautiful line of *Star Wars* ceramics around the time of *Return of the Jedi*. It's a C-3PO cellophane tape dispenser. On the dispenser, Threepio is in a terribly awkward position, supine with his knees raised in an arch, the roll of tape on a spindle between them. Convention crowds get a laugh when Tony Daniels describes the piece. "Imagine!" he says in mock horror. "You pull out the tape from between my legs. What an indignity!"

The list that follows is a comprehensive look at classic *Star Wars* trilogy collectibles that feature C-3PO by himself. Since Threepio was used in many works of fiction as comic relief, and paired with R2-D2 or other classic *Star Wars* characters on merchandise, any list that mentioned every appearance would itself likely be the size of this entire book.

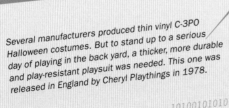

Several manufacturers produced thin vinyl C-3PO Halloween costumes. But to stand up to a serious day of playing in the back yard, a thicker, more durable and play-resistant playsuit was needed. This one was released in England by Cheryl Playthings in 1978.

Roman Ceramics produced this well-plated
C-3PO bank in 1978 as part of a line that
included R2-D2 and Darth Vader.

APPAREL

United States

C-3PO socks
Charleston Hosiery Mills, 1977

C-3PO T-shirt
Factors, 1977

C-3PO glitter T-shirt
Factors, 1977

C-3PO girl's Underoos
Union Underwear, 1980

ROTJ cuffed knit cap
Sales Corp. of America, 1983

C-3PO ROTJ black gloves
Sales Corp. of America, 1983

C-3PO ROTJ navy mittens
Sales Corp. of America, 1983

C-3PO ROTJ leg warmers
Sales Corp. of America, 1983

C-3PO ROTJ scarf
Sales Corp. of America, 1983

C-3PO parts identification sweatshirt
Uniprints, 1983

C-3PO SW Galaxy I (art by Joe Smith) T-shirt
American Marketing, 1994

C-3PO black and white stipple T-shirt
Changes, 1995

C-3PO vintage ringer T-shirt
Changes, 1996

Double-sided C-3PO/R2-D2 tie-dye T-shirt
Liquid Blue, 1996

Black T-shirt with C-3PO image on front
Changes, 1997

Australia

C-3PO bathrobe (C-3PO head)
Mr. Australia Garments, 1980

C-3PO bathrobe (C-3PO full figure)
Mr. Australia Garments, 1980

Canada

C-3PO's Cereal premium hat (mail-in)
Kellogg's, 1984

Mexico

C-3PO belt
Tudor Brand, 1980

BANKS/WALLETS

United States

C-3PO ceramic bank
Roman Ceramics, 1978

England

C-3PO change purse
Touchline Promotions, 1983

BED AND BATH

United States

C-3PO/R2-D2 reversible pillowcase (boxed)
Bibb, 1980

Darth Vader/C-3PO reversible pillowcase
WestPoint Stevens, 1997

C-3PO/R2-D2 reversible pillowcase
WestPoint Stevens, 1997

C-3PO bath towel
WestPoint Stevens, 1997

BOOKS AND RELATED

United States

C-3PO's Book about Robots, softcover
Random House, 1979

C-3PO bookmark
Random House, 1983

C-3PO tassel bookmark
Antioch, 1995

C-3PO shapemark bookmark
Antioch, 1996

Droids: The Kalarba Adventures hardcover comic collection
(limited, signed by Anthony Daniels)
Dark Horse Comics, 1996

Star Wars: The Magic of Myth, softcover (C-3PO cover)
Bantam, 1997

Star Wars: The Magic of Myth, hardcover (C-3PO cover)
Bantam, 1997

Spain

La Desaparacion de C-3PO pop-up book
1985

Get clean with the help of C-3PO bubble bath, shampoo, or this bar of sculpted soap from the British company Cliro in 1978.

BUTTONS

United States

3" C-3PO button
Factors, 1977

1.5" C-3PO button
SW Fan Club, 1978

C-3PO Droids Animated Classics button
Fox Video, 1996

England

2" C-3PO button
Touchline, 1983

2" C-3PO button with flashing eyes
Starfire, 1983

France

C-3PO and Protocol Droid button
Mister Badges, 1980

C-3PO button
Mister Badges, 1980

Germany

C-3PO button
APS Schumacher, 1983

Japan

2" SW C-3PO button (plastic)
Factors, 1977

C-3PO pin with light up eyes
Toho, 1997

The Netherlands

C-3PO and Protocol Droid button
Apple and Egg Productions, 1980

C-3PO button
Apple and Egg Productions, 1980

CERAMICS

United States

C-3PO ceramic metallic cookie jar
Roman Ceramics, 1977

C-3PO ceramic mug
Sigma, 1983

C-3PO ceramic pencil tray
Sigma, 1983

C-3PO ceramic tape dispenser
Sigma, 1983

C-3PO ceramic picture frame
Sigma, 1983

C-3PO in turret ceramic music box
Sigma, 1983

C-3PO ceramic mug
Applause, 1995

C-3PO ceramic cookie jar
Star Jars, 1998

COSTUMES

United States

SW Golden Robot (C-3PO) costume, black box
Ben Cooper, 1977

SW Golden Robot (C-3PO) costume, blue box
Ben Cooper, 1977

C-3PO "chrome" child's face mask
Ben Cooper, 1977

C-3PO gold painted child face mask
Ben Cooper, 1977

C-3PO playsuit
Ben Cooper, 1977

C-3PO poncho
Ben Cooper, 1977

C-3PO gold latex mask
Don Post, 1977

C-3PO black latex mask with gold paint
Don Post, 1978

C-3PO latex mask, LFL copyright
Don Post, 1979–84

ESB Golden Robot (C-3PO) costume
Ben Cooper, 1980

ROTJ Golden Robot (C-3PO) costume
Ben Cooper, 1983

C-3PO deluxe child's costume
Rubies, 1994

C-3PO value priced costume
Rubies, 1994

C-3PO PVC mask (child)
Rubies, 1995

C-3PO rubber mask
Rubies, 1995

C-3PO jumpsuit with PVC mask
Rubies, 1995

C-3PO jumpsuit with shoe covers and PVC mask
Rubies, 1995

C-3PO costume kit
Rubies, 1996

Left: Underoos are fun to wear! Or at least so Union Underwear told the world in 1980. Girls had a choice of three different Star Wars characters to wear, including C-3PO. But we thought he was a, um, he.

Antioch produced two bookmarks with C-3PO on them. One had a tassel and the other was this die-cut "shapemark" from 1996.

C-3PO PVC mask (adult)
Rubies, 1997

C-3PO miniature helmet
Riddell, 1997

AUSTRALIA

C-3PO costume
Croner Trading, 1980

BELGIUM

C-3PO costume
J.P. Belgium, 1980

ENGLAND

C-3PO playsuit
Cheryl Playthings, 1977

C-3PO costume
Acamas Toys, 1983

FRANCE

C-3PO child's face mask
Cesar, 1977

C-3PO adult's face mask
Cesar, 1977

C-3PO adult's pull-over mask
Cesar, 1977

JAPAN

C-3PO rubber pull-over mask
Ogawa-Gomu Co., 1983

MEXICO

C-3PO paper mask
Papeles Troquelados, 1980

C-3PO plastic mask
Creaciones Juanin, 1983

SPAIN

C-3PO Droids costume
Josman, 1984

SWITZERLAND

C-3PO mask
Urweider, 1977

COMPUTER RELATED

UNITED STATES

C-3PO mouse
American Covers, 1998

ENGLAND

C-3PO mouse pad (British Petroleum premium)
Pepsi, 1997

JAPAN

C-3PO die cut mouse pad
Amada, 1997

CRAFTS

UNITED STATES

C-3PO glitter iron-on
Factors, 1977

C-3PO iron-on with gold lettering
Factors, 1980

C-3PO iron-on with blue triangle logo
Factors, 1980

C-3PO iron-on with horizontal stripe with character name
Factors, 1980

C-3PO latch hook rug kit
Lee Wards, 1980

C-3PO sun catcher
Lee Wards, 1980

C-3PO rubber stamp
Adam Joseph, 1983

C-3PO figure rubber stamp
Rose Art, 1997

CUPS/GLASSES

UNITED STATES

Plastic drink cup with C-3PO poseable figure topper
KFC (Hawaii), 1997

Plastic drink cup with C-3PO poseable figure topper
FAO Schwarz (Las Vegas), 1997

C-3PO child's plastic mug
Applause, 1997

C-3PO medium drink cup
Taco Bell, 1997

*From Amada in Japan comes this unusual
1997 die-cut C-3PO mouse pad.*

110100101001001001010010100101111100

AUSTRALIA

C-3PO plastic tumbler
Pizza Hut, 1995

C-3PO frosted character glass
Crystal Craft, 1996

CANADA

Plastic drink cup with C-3PO poseable figure topper
Taco Bell, 1997

C-3PO medium drink cup
Taco Bell, 1997

THE NETHERLANDS

C-3PO drink cup
Pepsi, 1997

MEXICO

C-3PO cup with flex lid and straw
Pepsi, 1997

C-3PO sport bottle with blue lid and flex straw
Pepsi, 1997

C-3PO Pepsi glass
Pepsi, 1997

Slender C-3PO Pepsi glass
Pepsi, 1997

FILM, VIDEO, AND SLIDES

UNITED STATES

70mm C-3PO collectible film frame
Willitts, 1995

C-3PO freeze frame slide
Kenner, 1998

FOOD RELATED

UNITED STATES

C-3PO card #7 (of 16)
Wonder Bread, 1977

C-3PO stick-on from GM cereals
General Mills, 1977

Burger Chef C-3PO Funmeal droid puppet tray
Coke/Burger Chef, 1978

ESB C-3PO candy head
Topps, 1980

C-3PO's cereal box with Luke mask on back
Kellogg's, 1984

C-3PO's cereal box with Darth Vader mask on back
Kellogg's, 1984

C-3PO's cereal box with Stormtrooper mask on back
Kellogg's, 1984

C-3PO's cereal box with Yoda mask on back
Kellogg's, 1984

C-3PO's cereal box with C-3PO mask on back
Kellogg's, 1984

C-3PO's cereal box with Chewbacca mask on back
Kellogg's, 1984

C-3PO's cereal box with rocket ad
Kellogg's, 1984

C-3PO's cereal box with card/sticker ad
Kellogg's, 1984

Set of 10 stickers/trading cards from C-3PO cereal
Kellogg's, 1984

Set of 3 rebel rockets from C-3PO cereal
Kellogg's, 1984

Pepsi C-3PO 12-pack box
Pepsi, 1997

Pepsi C-3PO 24-pack box
Pepsi, 1997

C-3PO bagged PEZ (blue, red, or green)
PEZ, 1997

C-3PO carded PEZ
PEZ, 1997

C-3PO pizza take-out box
Pizza Hut, 1997

C-3PO paper food bag
Taco Bell, 1997

C-3PO paper food wrapper
Taco Bell, 1997

C-3PO peel-off game piece #6 from SW: Special Edition game
Taco Bell, 1997

Meet C-3PO at your local grocery store!
This life-size aisle display of the golden one
advertised Kellogg's C-3PO's cereal in 1984.

C-3PO Doritos chip bags (various sizes)
Frito Lay, 1997

C-3PO Cheetos chip bags (various sizes)
Frito Lay, 1997

AUSTRALIA

C-3PO carded bag of jelly candies
Red Tulip, 1980

C-3PO candy sucker
Red Tulip, 1980

C-3PO miniature and backdrop from kids meal
Pizza Hut, 1995

C-3PO carded PEZ
PEZ, 1997

C-3PO hologram Tazo #148
Frito Lay, 1997

BRAZIL

Brin-Q drink mix pack #11, C-3PO
Belavista, 1997

C-3PO mini candy card/wrapper #4
Freegels, 1997

CANADA

C-3PO's cereal box with Luke mask on back
Kellogg's, 1984

C-3PO's cereal box with Darth Vader mask on back
Kellogg's, 1984

C-3PO's cereal box with Stormtrooper mask on back
Kellogg's, 1984

C-3PO's cereal box with Yoda mask on back
Kellogg's, 1984

C-3PO's cereal box with C-3PO mask on back
Kellogg's, 1984

C-3PO's cereal box with sticker ad
Kellogg's, 1984

C-3PO's mini cereal box
Kellogg's, 1984

Set of 20 stickers/trading cards from C-3PO cereal
Kellogg's, 1984

C-3PO Pepsi 12-pack box
Pepsi, 1997

C-3PO carded PEZ
PEZ, 1997

ENGLAND

C-3PO SW popsicle wrapper
Lyons Maid, 1977

C-3PO punch out mask from ice cream packages
Lyons Maid, 1977

C-3PO candy head
Topps, 1997

Repair C-3PO magnetic puzzle
Taco Bell, 1997

C-3PO cookie bag
Burton's Biscuits, 1997

C-3PO Walker's chip bags (various sizes and flavors)
Frito Lay, 1997

FRANCE

ESB C-3PO yogurt card #2
Yoplait, 1980

GREECE

C-3PO bagged PEZ
PEZ, 1997

HONG KONG

C-3PO Sprite ruler
Coca Cola, 1980

INDONESIA

C-3PO film frame #2
Indofood, 1997

MEXICO

Fantasy Ball Lollipop with C-3PO packaging
Sonrics, 1997

C-3PO figurine from assorted cookie boxes
Gamesa, 1997

Emperador cookie wrapper with C-3PO on front
Gamesa, 1997

Polvorones cookie wrapper with C-3PO on front
Gamesa, 1997

Cookie boxes with C-3PO's image
Gamesa, 1997

C-3PO game piece #15 from assorted cookie packages
(3 different card backs)
Gamesa, 1997

"A new force at breakfast. Two cereal rings fused together!" The crossover of cereal box collecting with Star Wars makes the 1984 Kellogg's C-3PO's cereal boxes a cherished collectible. There were eight different boxes in the U.S., some with masks to cut out on back and others with trading cards or one of three different "rebel rockets" to collect.

THE NETHERLANDS

UFO's ESB round C-3PO sticker
Preservenbedrijj B.V., 1980

C-3PO bagged PEZ
PEZ, 1997

C-3PO sticker from PEZ refill pack
PEZ, 1997

NEW ZEALAND

C-3PO circular sticker from Twinkies
General Foods, 1980

C-3PO cutout paper mask from ice cream packages
Tip Top, 1980

SPAIN

C-3PO figurine from Tombola chocolate egg
Chupa Chups, 1997

Fantasy Ball Lollipop with C-3PO bag
Chupa Chups, 1997

C-3PO Port-a-Chup lollipop
Chupa Chups, 1997

C-3PO ice cream stick
Frigo, 1997

FOOTWEAR

UNITED STATES

C-3PO shoes, navy suede
Clarks, 1977

C-3PO shoes, brown suede
Clarks, 1977

C-3PO shoes, burgundy leather
Clarks, 1977

C-3PO shoes, black and gold fabric
Clarks, 1977

C-3PO sneakers, red canvas
Clarks, 1977

AUSTRALIA

C-3PO PVC thongs
Fairlane Investments, 1983

GAMES

UNITED STATES

C-3PO gaming miniature
West End Games, 1988

C-3PO black bordered Customizable Card Game card
Decipher, 1995

C-3PO white bordered Customizable Card Game card
Decipher, 1995

SW: Customizable Card Game C-3PO tournament deck box
Decipher, 1998

HOUSEHOLD AND KITCHEN RELATED

UNITED STATES

C-3PO flying disc
Pine Sol, 1978

C-3PO switcheroo
Kenner, 1980

C-3PO cake pan
Wilton Ent., 1980

C-3PO night-light
Adam Joseph, 1983

C-3PO dimensional night-light
Adam Joseph, 1983

C-3PO doorknob hanger
Antioch, 1996

C-3PO metallic holiday ornament
Neiman Marcus, 1997

C-3PO hand blown glass ornament
Christopher Radko, 1998

AUSTRALIA

C-3PO toothbrush holder
Crystal Craft, 1983

JAPAN

C-3PO and George Lucas telephone card
Panasonic, 1987 and 1988

C-3PO telephone card
Teleca, 1998

SPAIN

C-3PO mobile
Ediciones Manantial, 1978

Above: C-3PO masks were produced from the time that Star Wars was released in 1977, but how about a "shrunken" C-3PO head? Riddell, manufacturer of pro sports equipment, took its products to a much smaller scale with miniature sports helmets and then replica Star Wars helmets about 45% actual size. This C-3PO mini head has illuminated eyes that are triggered by a motion sensor in its mouth.

This 1978 C-3PO plastic play pendant from Japan's Patora seems rather large to wear around a young girl's neck.

JEWELRY

UNITED STATES

C-3PO barrette
Weingeroff, 1977

C-3PO bracelet
Weingeroff, 1977

C-3PO pierced earrings
Weingeroff, 1977

C-3PO clip-on earrings
Weingeroff, 1977

C-3PO key chain
Weingeroff, 1977

C-3PO small head pendant
Weingeroff, 1977

C-3PO large head pendant
Weingeroff, 1977

C-3PO ring
Weingeroff, 1977

C-3PO scatter pin
Weingeroff, 1977

C-3PO stick pin
Weingeroff, 1977

C-3PO bust pendant
Adam Joseph, 1983

C-3PO bust pin
Adam Joseph, 1983

C-3PO enameled pin
Howard Eldon, 1987

C-3PO pin
Hollywood Pins, 1995

C-3PO pin, "We're Doomed"
Hollywood Pins, 1995

C-3PO die-cast key chain (on blister card)
Placo Toys, 1996

C-3PO die-cast gold key chain (in box)
Placo Toys, 1996

CANADA

C-3PO die-cast key chain (on blister card)
Placo Toys, 1996

ENGLAND

C-3PO sterling silver pendant
Pastahurst Ltd., 1978

C-3PO gold pendant
Pastahurst Ltd., 1978

C-3PO sterling silver pin
Pastahurst Ltd., 1978

C-3PO gold pin
Pastahurst Ltd., 1978

JAPAN

C-3PO copper pin
Takara, 1977

C-3PO plastic pendant
Patora, 1978

C-3PO ring (silver)
J.A.P., 1997

C-3PO ring (24k gold)
J.A.P., 1997

C-3PO metal key holder
Banpresto, 1998

MODELS

UNITED STATES

C-3PO model kit, SW wide box
MPC, 1977

C-3PO model kit, SW narrow box
MPC, 1977

C-3PO model kit, ROTJ box
MPC, 1983

C-3PO wind-up Structors model kit
MPC, 1984

C-3PO 1/4 scale vinyl model kit
Screamin', 1994

C-3PO 1/6 scale vinyl model kit
Screamin', 1994

ENGLAND

C-3PO model kit
Denys Fisher, 1977

C-3PO wind-up Structors model kit
Airfix, 1984

FRANCE

Z-6PO (C-3PO) model kit
Meccano, 1977

*One of the strangest of all theatrical posters for
Star Wars is this stone-litho looking one from Poland
in the late 1970s.*

120

C-3PO: TALES OF THE GOLDEN DROID

GERMANY

C-3PO model kit, SW box
Kenner, 1977

JAPAN

C-3PO model kit
Revell/Takara, 1977

C-3PO model kit
Takara, 1977

C-3PO 1/6 scale resin model kit
Kaiyodo, 1993

C-3PO 1/6 scale vinyl model kit
Kaiyodo, 1993

PARTY ITEMS

AUSTRALIA

C-3PO giant balloon
Balloon Supply, 1983

ENGLAND

C-3PO balloon
Kiwi Products/Ariel, 1983

PEWTER

UNITED STATES

C-3PO chess piece
Danbury Mint, 1995

C-3PO pewter figurine
Rawcliffe, 1996

PLAQUES, SCULPTURES, AND LIMITED EDITIONS

UNITED STATES

ESB: C-3PO photo plaque signed by Anthony Daniels
Scoreboard, 1993

C-3PO life-size prop replica
Don Post, 1998

POSTERS

UNITED STATES

Star Wars Poster Monthly issue #5
with C-3PO foldout poster
Paradise Press, 1978

Star Wars radio dramatization poster, 17" x 29"
National Public Radio, 1981

Star Wars radio dramatization poster reprinted, 22" x 32"
Kilian Ent., 1995

C-3PO Pepsi poster
Pepsi, 1997

JAPAN

George Lucas and C-3PO
with butterfly net, 41" x 57"
Panasonic, 1988

George Lucas and C-3PO
with butterfly net, 29" x 40"
Panasonic, 1988

George Lucas and C-3PO
with butterfly net, 10 year logo, 14" x 40"
Panasonic, 1988

George Lucas and C-3PO
with butterfly net, pink top, 21" x 70" cloth
Panasonic, 1988

C-3PO silk-like cloth banner, red stripe
with Maclord logo, 19.5" x 35.5"
Panasonic, 1988

POLAND

Star Wars movie poster
with C-3PO and spotted yellow background
1977

SHOW SOUVENIRS

JAPAN

C-3PO PVC key chain
Kenneth Feld Pdns., 1992

STAMPS/COINS

UNITED STATES

C-3PO Power of the Force coin (silver tone)
Kenner, 1984

C-3PO Droids coin (gold tone)
Kenner, 1984

Left: Despite the droid's popularity, C-3PO was one of the last major characters to be produced as a pewter figurine from Rawcliffe in 1996.

Above: In 1998, Hasbro introduced a limited line of six-inch "Epic Force" figurines in poses from the films. This beautifully detailed and decorated C-3PO seems to be begging for help.

C-3PO Protocol Droid coin (gold tone)
Kenner, 1984

C-3PO Protocol Droid coin (gold tone)
Kenner, 1998

STANDEES

United States

C-3PO standee
Factors, 1977

C-3PO standee
Advanced Graphics, 1994

STAR TOURS

United States

C-3PO PVC figurine, light yellow
Disney, 1988

White ceramic mug with C-3PO design
Disney, 1990

White T-shirt with C-3PO schematic
Disney, 1990

C-3PO magnet
Disney, 1992

Plastic robot claw toy with C-3PO on packaging
Disney, 1992

C-3PO PVC figurine, gold colored
Disney, 1992

Round button with C-3PO and "Disneyland 35 Years of Magic"
Disney, 1992

Black T-shirt with C-3PO supergraphic head on front and back
Disney, 1993

White short sleeve cutoff T-shirt with artsy C-3PO
in green, yellow, and pink
Disney, 1994

France

White T-shirt with C-3PO schematic
Disney, 1990

C-3PO PVC figurine
Disney, 1992

Japan

White sweatshirt with metallic C-3PO design and
"Welcome to Tomorrowland Starport"
Disney, 1988

White T-shirt with yellow C-3PO on blue
Disney, 1988

Chrome telephone card with C-3PO and Starspeeder
Disney, 1992

C-3PO PVC figural key chain
Disney, 1992

Mini slide puzzle key chain of C-3PO and Starspeeder
Disney, 1993

STATIONERY/SCHOOL SUPPLIES

United States

C-3PO birthday card for 12-year-old
Drawing Board, 1977

C-3PO die cut birthday card
Drawing Board, 1977

C-3PO card, "Haven't Written"
Drawing Board, 1977

C-3PO card, "Rusty? Get well"
Drawing Board, 1977

C-3PO with Santa cap Christmas card
Drawing Board, 1977

C-3PO "Valentines Greeting" Valentine
Drawing Board, 1977

C-3PO with mask Halloween card
Drawing Board, 1977

C-3PO head glow-in-the-dark eraser
Butterfly Originals, 1983

C-3PO the "Thinker" birthday card
Drawing Board, 1983

Set of 2 markers on C-3PO blister card
Butterfly Originals, 1983

Gold pencil with C-3PO pattern
Butterfly Originals, 1983

Pencil with C-3PO topper
Butterfly Originals, 1983

Marker 2-pack on C-3PO card
Stuart Hall, 1983

C-3PO rectangular magnet
Ata Boy, 1995

Right: Because the droids weren't seen as humans, they were handy to use in promotions and advertising. This standee from Burger King in 1980 helped promote four different glasses decorated with characters and scenes from The Empire Strikes Back.

4" x 6" postcard, C-3PO in oil bath
Classico, 1995

4" x 6" postcard, C-3PO near *Falcon* controls
Classico, 1995

4" x 6" postcard, C-3PO (art by Joe Smith) SW Galaxy art
Classico, 1995

8" x 10" postcard, C-3PO in oil bath
Classico, 1995

C-3PO portfolio folder
Mead, 1997

AUSTRALIA

C-3PO ring binder
Reding Stationery, 1980

C-3PO card, "I like you"
Hallmark Australia Ltd., 1983

C-3PO puffy sticker
Crystal Craft, 1983

ENGLAND

C-3PO die cut eraser
Helix, 1978

C-3PO zippered pencil pouch
Helix, 1978

C-3PO exercise book pad
Letraset, 1978

C-3PO flat eraser
H.C. Ford, 1983

C-3PO head sticker, flat
Fun Products, 1983

C-3PO head sticker, vacu-formed
Fun Products, 1983

C-3PO prism sticker
Fun Products, 1983

GERMANY

C-3PO 4" x 6" postcard
Filmwelt Vertrieb, 1996

ITALY

C-3PO head sticker
Sodecor, 1983

JAPAN

C-3PO figural eraser, various colors
Maruka Toy Co., 1978

C-3PO stencil (green, yellow, red, or blue)
Maruka Toy Co., 1978

C-3PO cloth pencil case
Sun Star Stationery, 1987

Mechanical pencil with C-3PO head on top
Showa Note, 1997

Pen with C-3PO head on top
Showa Note, 1997

C-3PO head on a tiny suction cup
Showa Note, 1997

STORE DISPLAYS

UNITED STATES

C-3PO 3-D book bin floor dump
Random House, 1983

C-3PO's cereal standee
Kellogg's, 1984

C-3PO's cereal folding sign, "A New Force at Breakfast"
Kellogg's, 1984

C-3PO's cereal plastic shelf talker
Kellogg's, 1984

C-3PO bin standee for paperback books
Bantam, 1994

C-3PO SW: Special Edition Pepsi standee
Pepsi, 1997

JAPAN

C-3PO die cut standee
Panasonic, 1988

Lucas and C-3PO mini die cut shelf standee
Panasonic, 1988

TOILETRIES

UNITED STATES

C-3PO soap
Omni Cosmetics, 1981

CANADA

C-3PO soap
Omni Cosmetics, 1981

ENGLAND

C-3PO sculpted soap
Cliro, 1978

C-3PO bath gel
Addis, 1984

C-3PO bubble bath
Addis, 1984

Left: Take a break from doing your home or office work and listen to four different recorded Threepio phrases with the C-3PO FX Pen from Tiger Electronics, produced in 1997. Just don't let your teacher—or boss—hear it and confiscate it.

Above: C-3PO appears on many school supplies, from pencils and pens to magnets and binders. This zippered pencil pouch was produced in England by Helix in 1978.

TOYS: ACTION FIGURES, DOLLS, AND RELATED

United States

C-3PO action figure (SW card)
Kenner, 1978

C-3PO large-size action figure
Kenner, 1978

C-3PO action figure (ESB card)
Kenner, 1980

C-3PO action figure with removable limbs (ESB card)
Kenner, 1982

C-3PO action figure with removable limbs (ROTJ card)
Kenner, 1983

C-3PO action figure collector case
Kenner, 1984

C-3PO action figure (Power of the Force card)
Kenner, 1984

C-3PO action figure with Droids coin (Droids card)
Kenner, 1984

C-3PO action figure with Protocol Droid coin (Droids card)
Kenner, 1984

C-3PO action figure (orange card)
Kenner, 1995

C-3PO talking action figure carry case
Kenner, 1996

C-3PO action figure (green card)
Kenner, 1997

C-3PO collector series 12" doll
Kenner, 1997

C-3PO action figure with removable limbs (freeze frame card)
Kenner, 1998

C-3PO action figure with Millennium Minted coin
Kenner, 1998

C-3PO action figure (Flashback Photo card)
Kenner, 1999

Brazil

C-3PO action figure
Glassite, 1988

C-3PO Droids action figure
Glassite, 1988

Canada

C-3PO action figure (SW card)
Kenner Canada, 1978

C-3PO action figure (ESB card)
Kenner Canada, 1980

C-3PO action figure with removable limbs (ESB card)
Kenner Canada, 1982

C-3PO action figure with removable limbs (ROTJ card)
Kenner Canada, 1983

C-3PO action figure with Droids coin (Droids card)
Kenner Canada, 1984

C-3PO action figure with protocol droid coin (Droids card)
Kenner Canada, 1984

C-3PO action figure (orange card)
Kenner Canada, 1995

C-3PO action figure (green card)
Kenner Canada, 1997

C-3PO collector series 12" doll
Kenner Canada, 1997

C-3PO action figure with removable limbs (freeze frame card)
Kenner Canada, 1998

C-3PO action figure (Flashback Photo card)
Kenner Canada, 1999

England

C-3PO action figure (SW card)
Palitoy, 1978

C-3PO action figure (ESB card)
Palitoy, 1980

C-3PO action figure with removable limbs (ESB card)
Palitoy, 1982

C-3PO action figure with removable limbs (ROTJ card)
Palitoy, 1983

C-3PO action figure with removable limbs (tri-logo card)
Palitoy, 1984

C-3PO collector series 12" doll
Kenner, 1997

Left: The original 12-inch "See-Threepio" large action figure was sold all over the world in the late 1970s. This version is from England's Denys Fisher.

Below: Being one of the most popular characters on screen also led to popularity on a smaller scale, about 3 inches. Kenner and its affiliates, such as England's Palitoy, produced hundreds of thousands of C-3PO action figures over the years.

01010010010010010101001
00100010010100010011100101100100110001

FRANCE

SW carded Z-6PO (C-3PO) action figure
Meccano, 1978

Large size Z-6PO action figure
Meccano, 1979

GERMANY

SW carded C-3PO action figure
General Mills, 1978

ITALY

SW carded (C-3PO) action figure
Harbert, 1978

JAPAN

C-3PO 8" action figure
Takara, 1978

C-3PO action figure (SW card)
Takara, 1978

C-3PO die cast action figure
Takara, 1978

ESB boxed C-3PO action figure in box #4
Popy, 1980

C-3PO action figure with removable limbs (ROTJ card)
Tsukuda, 1983

C-3PO action figure, greenish tint (orange card)
Hasbro Japan, 1995

C-3PO action figure (orange card)
Hasbro Japan, 1995

C-3PO action figure (green card)
Hasbro Japan, 1997

C-3PO action figure with removable limbs (freeze frame card)
Hasbro Japan, 1998

C-3PO action figure (Flashback Photo card)
Hasbro Japan

MEXICO

C-3PO action figure with removable limbs (ROTJ card)
Lily-Ledy, 1983

TOYS: ELECTRONIC

UNITED STATES

C-3PO squawk box (carded)
Tiger, 1997

C-3PO squawk box (blister carded)
Tiger, 1997

C-3PO FX pen
Tiger, 1997

C-3PO flashlight key chain
Tiger, 1997

TOYS: MICRO MACHINE RELATED

UNITED STATES

Micro Machines C-3PO/Cantina transforming head playset
Galoob, 1995

Micro Machines mini-transforming head playset
(Wal-Mart mail order)
Galoob, 1997

CANADA

Micro Machines C-3PO/Cantina transforming head playset
Galoob, 1995

TOYS: MISCELLANEOUS

UNITED STATES

C-3PO Bend Em (form-fitting bubble)
Just Toys, 1993

C-3PO Bend Em with Topps trading card
(form-fitting bubble)
Just Toys, 1993

C-3PO Bend Em (square bubble)
Just Toys, 1993

C-3PO vinyl doll
Dakin, 1993

C-3PO Action Masters figurine
Kenner, 1994

C-3PO gold toned Action Masters mail order
Kenner, 1994

C-3PO PVC figurine
Applause, 1996

Epic Force C-3PO
Kenner, 1998

C-3PO vinyl doll
Applause, 1998

C-3PO Buddy small plush doll
Kenner, 1998

Left: In 1978 Japan's Takara produced a small line of three different die-cast Star Wars figures. The C-3PO figure actually fires rockets from his stomach launcher, a scene most of us evidently missed in the film.

Above: The Droids animated television series lasted only one season in 1985, but that was long enough for Kenner to produce a small line of figures, including this example of one of the series leads.

CANADA

C-3PO Action Masters figurine (orange card)
Kenner Canada, 1994

C-3PO Action Masters figurine (green carded)
Kenner Canada, 1997

C-3PO Buddy small plush doll
Kenner Canada, 1998

Epic Force C-3PO
Kenner Canada, 1998

JAPAN

C-3PO space alloy toy
Takara, 1978

Baby C-3PO small plush doll
Takara, 1992

Wind-up C-3PO tin toy
Osaka Tin Toy Institute, 1997

SPAIN

C-3PO PVC figurine
Comics Figuras, 1988

TRADING CARDS

UNITED STATES

C-3PO "X-rated" trading card #207
Topps, 1977

C-3PO corrected trading card #207
Topps, 1977

Classic Toys trading card #56, C-3PO action figure
1993

Action Master C-3PO trading card (3PO in oil bath)
Kenner, 1994

Action Master C-3PO trading card (3PO near *Falcon* controls)
Kenner, 1994

Die cast collectibles C-3PO trading card
Kenner, 1995

ENGLAND

Topps C-3PO card #8 from candy heads
Topps, 1995

ITALY

Vacu-formed C-3PO trading card Z6-Po (C-3PO)
Papou et Palmito, 1980

WATCHES AND CLOCKS

UNITED STATES

C-3PO hologram watch
Third Dimension Arts, 1993

C-3PO collector's sculpted watch, carded
Hope Ind., 1996

C-3PO collector's sculpted watch with *Falcon* case
Hope Ind., 1997

C-3PO collector's sculpted watch on smaller bubble package
Hope Ind., 1998

AUSTRALIA

C-3PO flip top watch (space battle card)
Playworks, 1996

C-3PO flip top watch (C-3PO card)
Playworks, 1997

CANADA

C-3PO flip top watch
Watchit, 1997

ENGLAND

Digital with C-3PO bust on orange background,
purple case, R2 and 3PO on strap
Watchit, 1997

C-3PO flip top watch
Watchit, 1997

Right: From the first watches in late 1977, C-3PO has graced children's and adults' hands while marking the time. This 1997 Watchit C-3PO digital watch from Australia is one of several recent timepieces featuring the golden droid.

Opposite: Entering the pantheon of Hollywood stars, C-3PO prints his name in wet cement near his just-impressed footprints at Mann's Chinese Theater in Los Angeles. Helping him with the task is none other than Star Wars *Producer Gary Kurtz.*

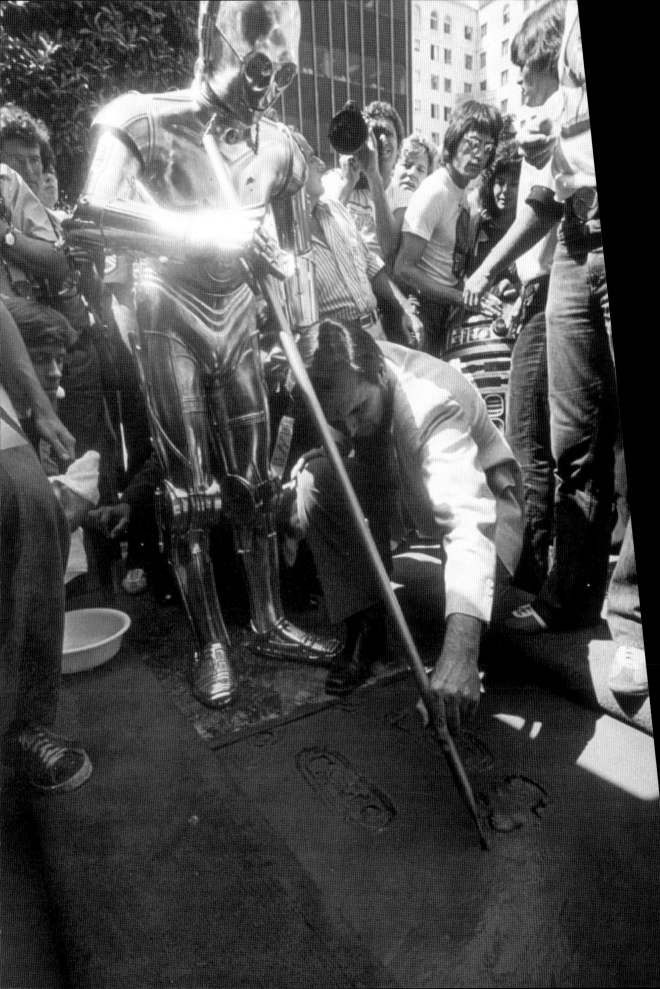

BIBLIOGRAPHY

I.   THE BIRTH OF THE GOLDEN DROID
     American Cinematographer *Star Wars* issue. July 1977.
     Bouzereau, Laurent. *Star Wars: The Annotated Screenlays*. New York: Del Rey Books, 1997.
     Brooks, Terry. *Star Wars:* Episode I *The Phantom Menace*. New York: Del Rey Books, 1999.
     Lippincott, Charles. Transcripts of unpublished interviews of George Lucas, Gary Kurtz, Ben Burtt, John Barry,
          Richard Chew, Norman Reynolds, and Anthony Daniels. San Anselmo, Calif.: Lucasfilm Ltd., 1977–78.
     Paley, Jane. Script for audio tour for *Star Wars: The Magic of Myth*. Produced by Visible Interactive.
          San Francisco, 1997.
     Sansweet, Stephen J. *Star Wars: From Concept to Screen to Collectible*. San Francisco: Chronicle Books, 1992.

II: THE SAGA OF SEE-THREEPIO
     Anderson, Kevin J. *The Jedi Academy* trilogy. New York: Bantam Books, 1994.
     Anderson, Kevin J. and Rebecca Moesta. *The Young Jedi Knights* series.
          New York: Berkley Publishing Group, 1995–1998.
     Austin, Terry, adaptor. *Splinter of the Mind's Eye* by Alan Dean Foster. Milwaukie, Oreg: Dark Horse Comics, 1995–96.
     Brooks, Terry, ibid.
     Daley, Brian. *The Empire Strikes Back*. Dramatizations for National Public Radio, 1983.
     ____. *The Empire Strikes Back*. Collected scripts from National Public Radio dramatization.
          New York: Del Rey Books, 1995.
     ____. *Return of the Jedi*. Dramatizations for National Public Radio, 1996.
     ____. *Return of the Jedi*. Collected scripts from National Public Radio dramatization. New York: Del Rey Books, 1996.
     ____. *Star Wars*. Dramatizations for National Public Radio, 1981.
     ____. *Star Wars*. Collected scripts from National Public Radio dramatization. New York: Del Rey Books, 1994.
     Droids: The Kalarba Adventures, Rebellion, Season of Revolt, and *The Protocol Offensive*.
          Milwaukie, Oreg: Dark Horse Comics, 1994–1997.
     Droids animated series, episodes 1–13. Toronto, Ont.: Nelvana, 1985.
     Foster, Alan Dean. *Splinter of the Mind's Eye*. New York: Del Rey Books, 1978.
     Glut, Donald F. *The Empire Strikes Back*. New York: Del Rey Books, 1980.
     Goodwin, Archie and Al Williamson. *Classic Star Wars* nos. 1–20. Milwaukie, Oreg: Dark Horse Comics, 1992–94.
     Kahn, James. *Return of the Jedi*. New York: Del Rey Books, 1983.
     Kube-McDowell, Michael P. *The Black Fleet Crisis* trilogy. New York: Bantam Books, 1996–97.
     Lucas, George. *Star Wars: A New Hope*. New York: Del Rey Books, 1976.
     Perry, Steve. *Shadows of the Empire*. New York: Bantam Books, 1996.
     Star Wars, nos. 1–107. New York: Marvel Comics, 1977–1986.
     Star Wars: A New Hope. 20th Century Fox, 1977.
     Star Wars: The Empire Strikes Back. Lucasfilm Ltd., 1980.
     Star Wars: Return of the Jedi. Lucasfilm Ltd., 1983.
     Star Wars: Episode I *The Phantom Menace*. Lucasfilm Ltd., 1999.
     Tyers, Kathy. *The Truce at Bakura*. New York: Bantam Books, 1993.
     Wolverton, Dave. *The Courtship of Princess Leia*. New York: Bantam Books, 1994.

III: GOLDEN TREASURES: C-3PO COLLECTIBLES
     Sansweet, Stephen J. and T.N. Tumbusch. *Tomart's Price Guide to Worldwide Star Wars Collectibles*, 2nd ed.
          Dayton, Ohio: Tomart Publications, 1997.